HOW TO USE THIS BOOK

MW00610039

HELP WITH THE DIAGRAMS

If this is your first paperfolding book purchase, here are a couple of things to help you.

Make sure your starting paper is square. Commercially available packs can normally be relied upon with respect to this.

You will find it helpful to use paper which has a colored and a white side. This helps to match the color shading in the diagrams. Paperfolding has its own international language which is written in symbols. Don't worry, there are only a handful of symbols and this book contains only a few of them.

Look at the first diagram step and figure out what should move where (the Symbols Section will be your first port of call). When you've sorted it out, make the fold. Compare your result with the next diagram step. If it matches, then move on to the next step and repeat this process. If it does not match, go back to the earlier step and try again.

The clues, in order of importance, are color, fold indication, direction of movement. Look at extra symbols, i.e., repeat, rotation, turn over, open out, and especially important, the inside reverse fold.

Be sure to familiarize yourself with these symbols and further information in the Symbols Section or you will find these diagrams more difficult to follow.

FOLDING ACCURACY

The best results come from accurate folding. The vast majority of models are, however, fairly forgiving in that small inaccuracies will not prevent an acceptable result. Don't worry too much about making a neat first model. The second attempt can always be better.

ABOUT THE MODELS

All the models in this book are of the same level of difficulty. They are classed as low intermediate. Once the inside reverse fold has been mastered then all are achievable. What do you do with the models when you are done? Display them, enjoy them, give them away. The choice is yours.

INTRODUCTION

FURTHER EXPLORATIONS

Explore what happens to a model if the number of units is reduced.

Explore the use of papers with different patterns.

Explore what happens if the final locking folds are taken alternately to front or back in Celtic series models.

Explore the aerodynamic properties of the models.

The joining method for units is called a lock. Explore the locks of a model from each series. What properties does a lock need? How do the locks differ?

Fold one unit from each family, then unfold and compare them. What features contribute to the final model?

CREATIVITY

You have the freedom to experiment with choice of paper size, type and color. In developing the models the author used 3 inch, 2 inch and later 1 inch squares. Most of the units are versatile and there are other variations as yet undiscovered. Feel free to use the models in this book as your starting point for further experiments.

USES FOR THE MODELS

Decorative photo frames, holiday wreaths, jewelry, gift decorations, greeting card decorations, etc. There is an abundance of possibilities. At the heart of all paperfolding is the joy of sharing a model made with your own hands.

ADVANTAGES OF PAPERFOLDING FOR TEACHERS AND PUPILS

The practical: a craft using no glue, no sharp scissors, no messy paints or crayons. Cheap working materials. High success rate. Attention-grabbing results. Non- competitive activity.

The cerebral: generally paperfolding evokes a non-threatening environment within which many skills can be fostered, i.e., development of hand-eye coordination and motor skills. Increased visual awareness. Increased mathematical awareness. Hands-on understanding of geometrical principles. Development of self confidence and self reliance. Development of self-working or team-working skills.

ORIGAMI WREATHS
AND RINGS

by David Petty

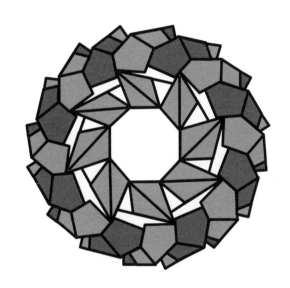

ZENAGRAF   Ann Arbor, Michigan

ORIGAMI WREATHS AND RINGS

Library of Congress Catalog Card Number: 98-61606
ISBN 0-9627254-1-2

Published by ZENAGRAF
Ann Arbor, Michigan

PREFACE

Sometime in the 1950's the art of origami, then mostly centered in Japan, enjoyed an explosion of popularity in England, the U.S. and all across Europe and into South America.

For several hundred years mothers in Japan have taught their children origami to amuse and exercise young fingers, while also teaching traditional folds. Now children the world over share their folded paper toys with friends. Many adults also teach each other and explore whole new areas of possibility in a simple square of paper.

In the 20th century Japanese master Akira Yoshizawa did much to popularize origami with his original designs and uses of paper that surpassed much of what came before. His work was little known in the West until his models were shown in exhibition in Amsterdam and New York. He also developed a diagramming system using symbols to stand for the basic origami operations.

These symbols have become adopted internationally. Lillian Oppenheimer from New York, a pioneer paperfolder of the first generation of modern American paperfolders, began to spread the magic of origami far and wide, introducing Yoshizawa and others from around the world as well as creating The Origami Center which has grown into the non-profit organization Origami U.S.A.

During this period much was uncovered from earlier times. Notably, the German educator Friedrich Fröbel developed origami lessons for his Kindergarten as both manual training and development of math skills.

Paperfolding has always been popular with children wherever it has been introduced. Teachers using origami in the classroom have watched in wonder at the unleashing of the intuitive powers of a child's mind as a mistake in folding became a creative unfolding and inventive exploration.

Along with the introduction of brightly colored square paper following World War II, the visual enjoyment of folding paper continued to grow. The social aspects of sharing the joys of origami without language or cultural barrier bring this ancient craft firmly into the present day.

In the last 20 years origami has been increasingly taught both in and beyond the school system and is now used extensively in educational and therapeutic settings. The process of paperfolding is an enjoyable way to develop fine motor skills as well as careful listening and patience. It also promotes self esteem and pleasure in the completion of a marvelous result.

This highly motiviating craft lends itself to the teaching of form and symmetry as well as mathematics. There are many wonderful origami models which have been created by paperfolders from around the world, from intricate animals and decorative flowers to delightful boxes and complex modular geometrics. Modular origami or unit folding makes use of multiple units which fit together like a puzzle. This book by David Petty from England contains models suitable for beginning folders who are motivated to follow his clear instructions and discover the pleasures of modular folding.

TABLE OF CONTENTS

INTRODUCTION: HOW TO USE THIS BOOK - page 1

SYMBOLS - page 4

1 : Celtic Brooches - page 7

2 : Celtic Garlands - page 36

3 : Celtic Motifs - page 40

4 : Crane Wreaths - page 62

5 : Star Garlands - page 74

6 : Stars and Wreaths - page 80

7 : Modular Constructions - page 91

8 : Modular Rings - page 93

9 : Origami Math Lesson - page 115

BIOGRAPHIES - page 121

RESOURCES - page 123

Look for these icons at the foot of each page of a chapter

TEACHING ORIGAMI

Here are some commonsense tips if you want to demonstrate or teach paperfolding.

Prepare in advance. Fold several models and choose the best suited. If there is extra time you will be prepared with a second and third.

Fold the chosen model and learn all the moves. Practice teaching a friend, even if you are familiar with the model.

Ensure you have enough paper of the correct size for your students.

Use a large demonstration paper of a suitable color. For instance, Dayglo colored paper is readily visible, but rapidly tires the eyes, so is unsuitable. The creases should be easily seen by all the students.

Use a 9 inch or 10 inch sheet to make your folds so all students can see what you are doing. Mark fold lines with a marker pen, if necessary, or use a blackboard to talk about mountain and valley folds and difficult points.

Arrange the room so that all can see. The author favors a "U" shaped arrangement of desks or tables. The demonstrator should stand in the open top of the "U". This enables all the students' work to be seen at a glance and gives easy access to any strugglers.

Check the lighting. It should be light enough to see with no bright spots. Don't stand with a window behind you on a sunny day, for instance. At the start of the session, ask the students what experience, if any, they have of paperfolding. Seasoned folders can be used to help less experienced students.

Keep checking the progress of the students. Advance at the pace of the slowest.

As far as is humanly possible, help every student to get a result.

Avoid singling out individuals. Repeat a move if you see any who don't understand the first time. Use the formula "That was a more difficult move, I will repeat it, in case someone did not follow it" or similar.

Try to use descriptive language for each move. Avoid vague references like "fold from here to there". Rather use full references like "fold the top left corner so it touches the bottom right corner".

Encourage neatness and accuracy, but don't overstress the point.

Enjoy the experience. If you enjoy the session, so will most students.

SYMBOLS

SYMBOL	EXAMPLE	RESULT	FURTHER INFORMATION

**mountain fold
(dash - dot)**

— · — · — · —

arrows show
direction of
movement

half hidden arrow
means fold behind

**valley fold
(dash - dash)**

— — — —

turn over

**fold and
return**

or

a thin line shows
an existing crease

it is not an
instruction

**drawing scale
increase**

SYMBOL	EXAMPLE	RESULT	FURTHER INFORMATION

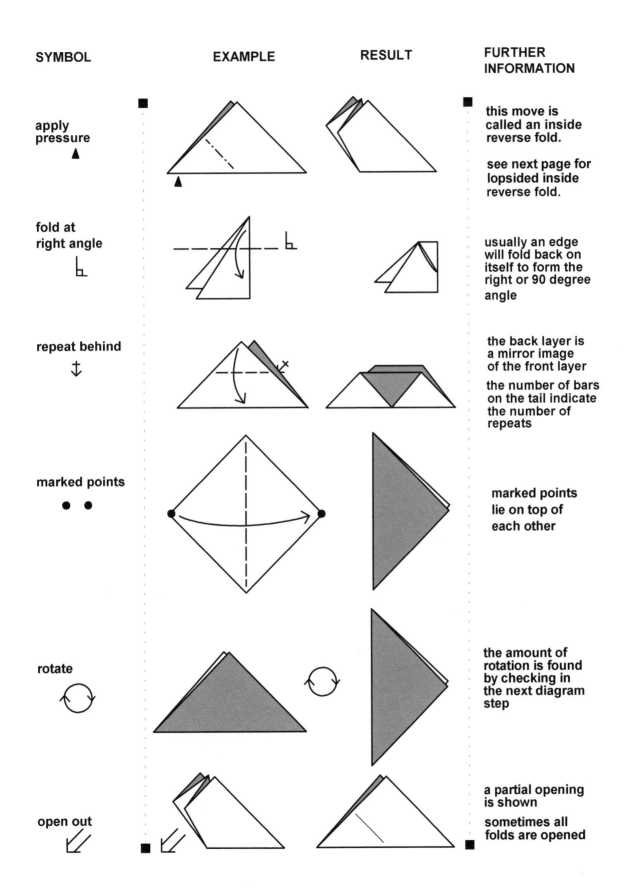

apply pressure
▲

this move is called an inside reverse fold.

see next page for lopsided inside reverse fold.

fold at right angle

usually an edge will fold back on itself to form the right or 90 degree angle

repeat behind

the back layer is a mirror image of the front layer

the number of bars on the tail indicate the number of repeats

marked points
● ●

marked points lie on top of each other

rotate

the amount of rotation is found by checking in the next diagram step

open out

a partial opening is shown

sometimes all folds are opened

SYMBOLS

LOPSIDED INSIDE REVERSE FOLD

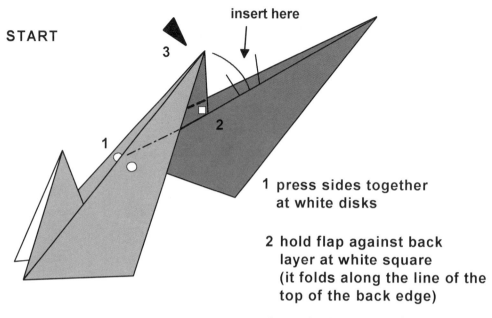

START

insert here

3

2

1

1 press sides together
 at white disks

2 hold flap against back
 layer at white square
 (it folds along the line of the
 top of the back edge)

3 push the whole flap inside

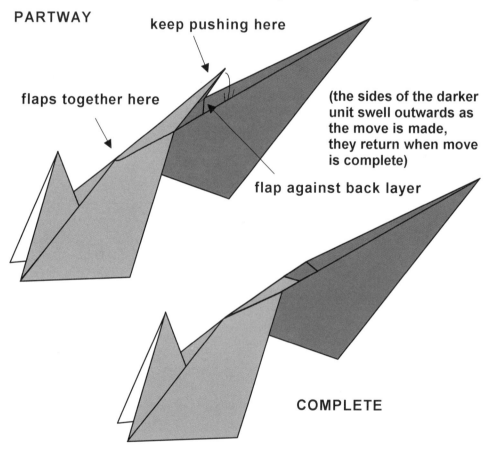

PARTWAY

keep pushing here

flaps together here

(the sides of the darker
unit swell outwards as
the move is made,
they return when move
is complete)

flap against back layer

COMPLETE

CELTIC BROOCH UNIT 1

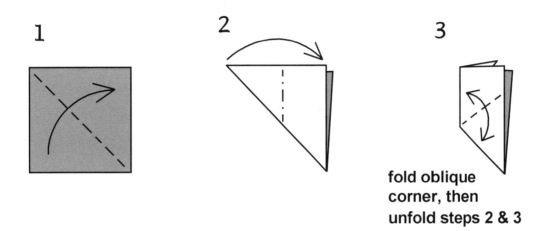

1

2

3

fold oblique
corner, then
unfold steps 2 & 3

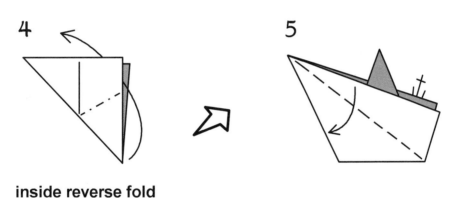

4

inside reverse fold

5

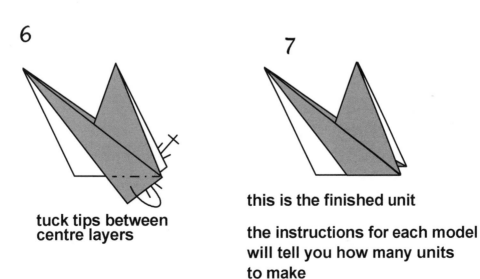

6

tuck tips between
centre layers

7

this is the finished unit

the instructions for each model
will tell you how many units
to make

CELTIC BROOCH 1

Use Celtic Brooch Unit 1 page 7   make 12 units

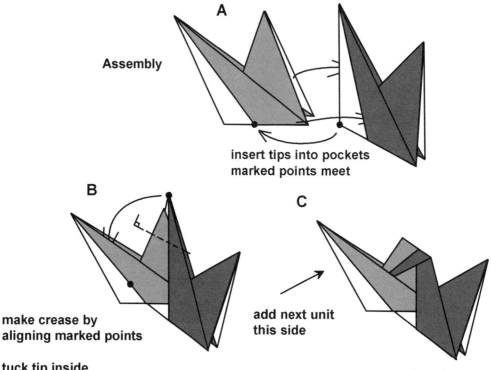

A

Assembly

insert tips into pockets
marked points meet

B

make crease by
aligning marked points

tuck tip inside

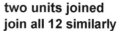

C

add next unit
this side

two units joined
join all 12 similarly

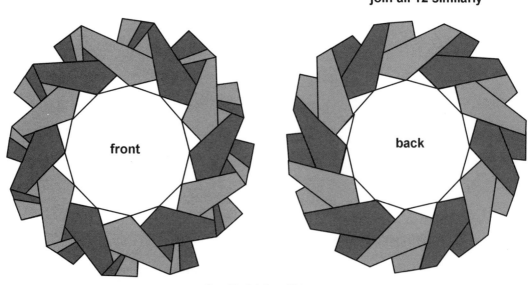

front

back

©   Model Jose Meeusen

©   Diagrams David Petty

CELTIC BROOCH 2

Use Celtic Brooch Unit 1 page 7   make 10 units

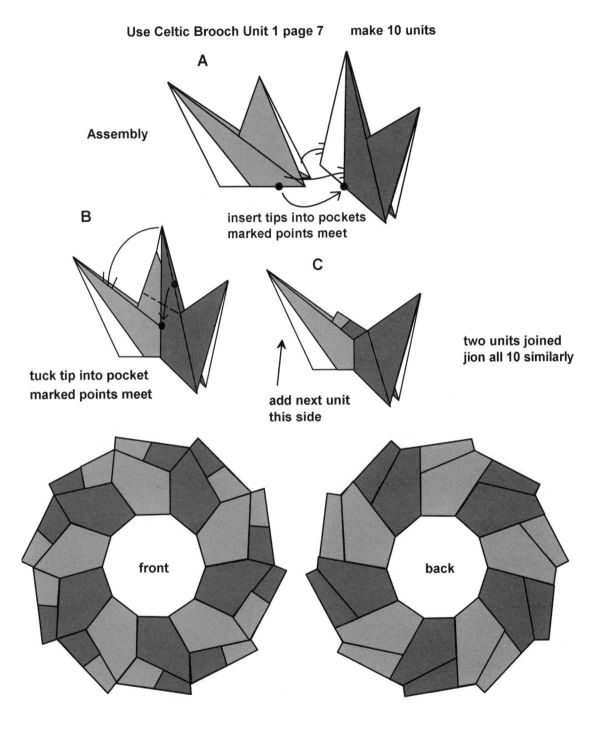

A

Assembly

insert tips into pockets
marked points meet

B

tuck tip into pocket
marked points meet

C

add next unit
this side

two units joined
jion all 10 similarly

front   back

© Model Jose Meeusen

© Diagrams David Petty

CELTIC BROOCH 3

Use Celtic Brooch Unit 1 page 7   **make 12 units**

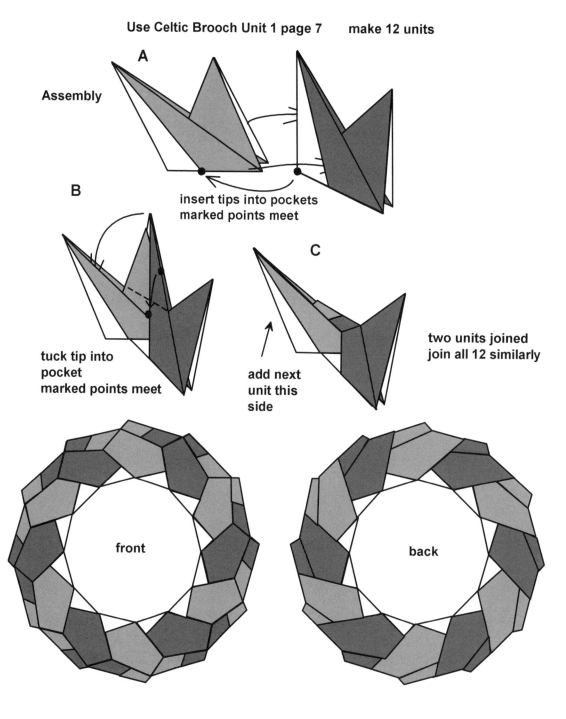

A

Assembly

insert tips into pockets
marked points meet

B

tuck tip into
pocket
marked points meet

C

add next
unit this
side

two units joined
join all 12 similarly

front

back

© Model Jose Meeusen

© Diagrams David Petty

CELTIC BROOCH 4

Use Celtic Brooch Unit 1 page 7   make 12 units

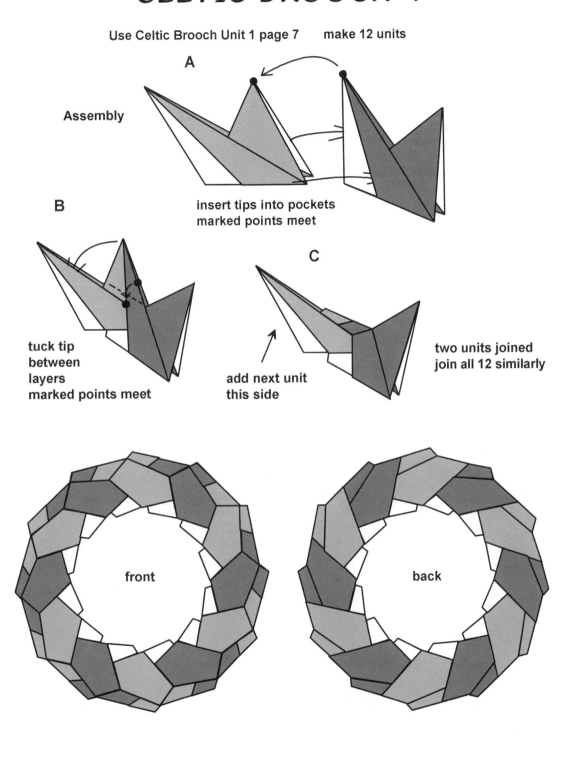

A

Assembly

insert tips into pockets
marked points meet

B

tuck tip
between
layers
marked points meet

C

add next unit
this side

two units joined
join all 12 similarly

front

back

© Model Jose Meeusen

© Diagrams David Petty

11   1: CELTIC BROOCHES

CELTIC BROOCH 5

Use Celtic Brooch Unit 1 page 7   make 12 units

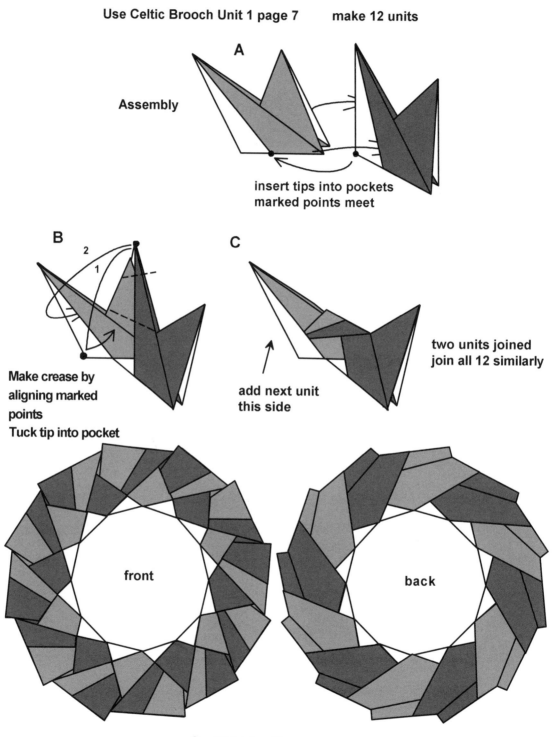

A

Assembly

insert tips into pockets
marked points meet

B

2

1

Make crease by
aligning marked
points
Tuck tip into pocket

C

add next unit
this side

two units joined
join all 12 similarly

front

back

©   Model Jose Meeusen

©   Diagrams David Petty

1: CELTIC BROOCHES   12

CELTIC BROOCH 6

Use Celtic Brooch Unit 1 page 7   **make 10 units**

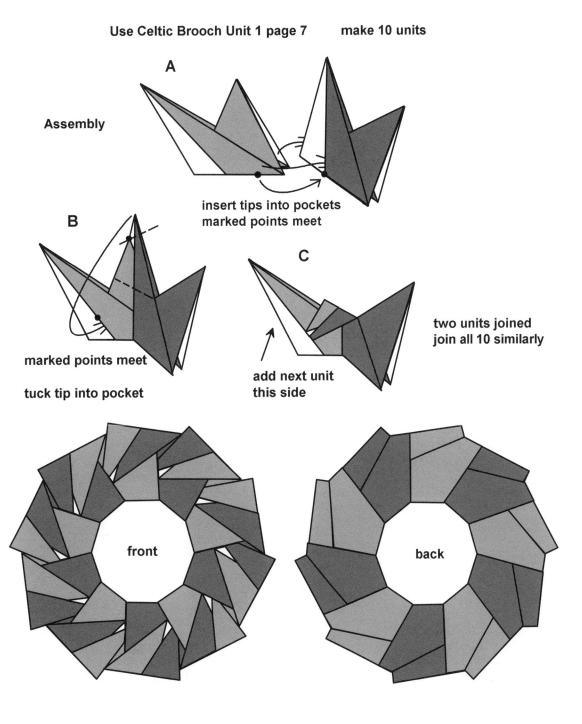

A

Assembly

insert tips into pockets
marked points meet

B

marked points meet

tuck tip into pocket

C

two units joined
join all 10 similarly

add next unit
this side

front

back

© **Model Jose Meeusen**

© **Diagrams David Petty**

CELTIC BROOCH 7

Use Celtic Brooch Unit 1 page 7   make 12 units

A

Assembly

insert tips into pockets
marked points meet

B

tuck tip
under

C

add next unit
this side

two units joined
join all 12 similarly

front

back

©   Model Jose Meeusen

©   Diagrams David Petty

CELTIC BROOCH UNIT 2

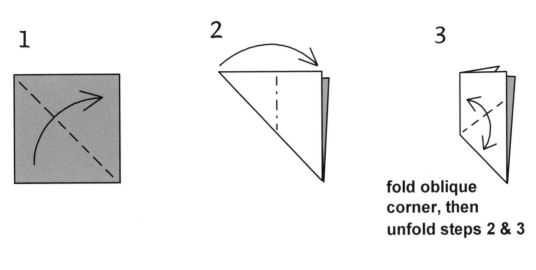

1

2

3

fold oblique
corner, then
unfold steps 2 & 3

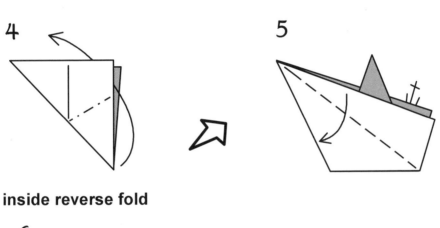

4

5

inside reverse fold

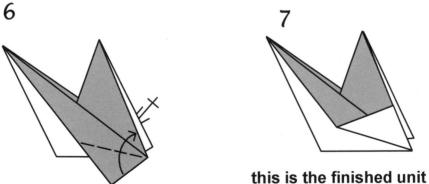

6

7

this is the finished unit

the instructions for each model
will tell you how many units
to make

1: CELTIC BROOCHES

CELTIC BROOCH 8

Use Celtic Brooch Unit 2 page 15   make 12 units

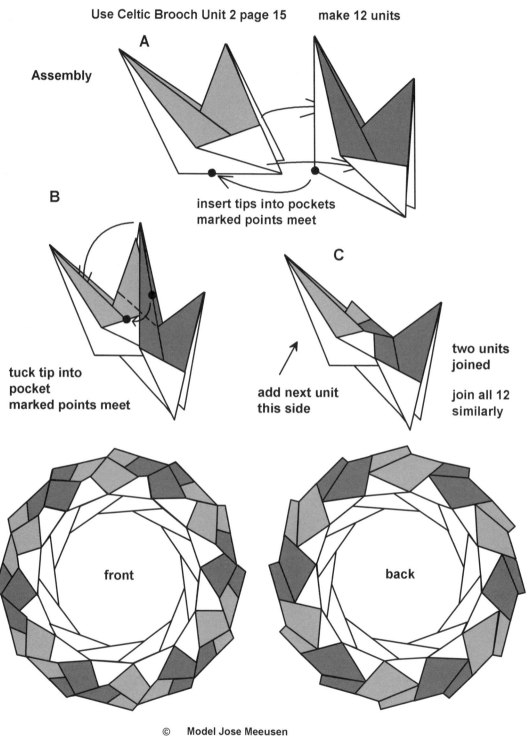

A

Assembly

insert tips into pockets
marked points meet

B

tuck tip into
pocket
marked points meet

C

add next unit
this side

two units
joined

join all 12
similarly

front   back

©   Model Jose Meeusen

©   Diagrams David Petty

CELTIC BROOCH 9

Use Celtic Brooch Unit 2 page 15   make 12 units

A

Assembly

insert tips into pockets
marked points meet

B

fold tip to align
with white edge
tuck tip inside

C

add next unit
this side

two units joined
join all 12 units
similarly

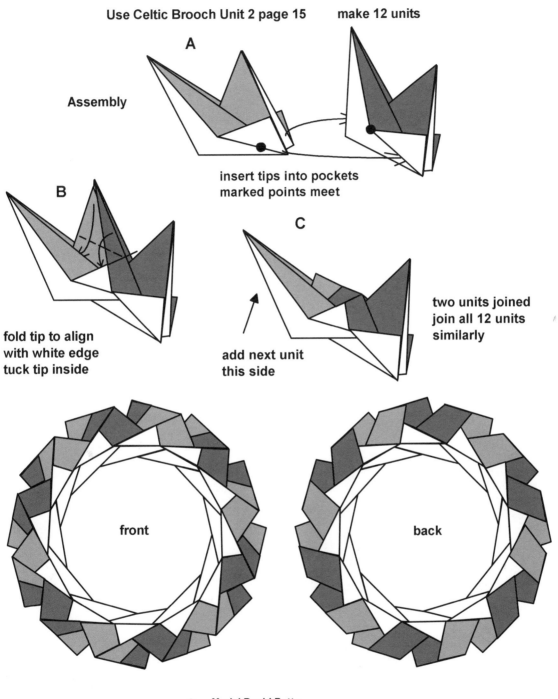

front

back

©   Model David Petty

©   Diagrams David Petty

CELTIC BROOCH 10

Assembly   Use Celtic Brooch Unit 2 page 15   make 10 units

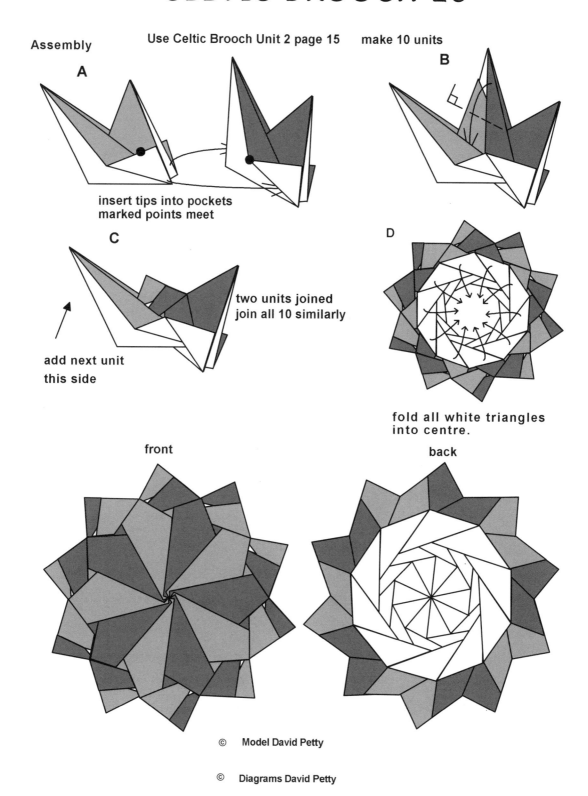

A

B

insert tips into pockets
marked points meet

C

two units joined
join all 10 similarly

add next unit
this side

D

fold all white triangles
into centre.

front

back

CELTIC BROOCH UNIT 3

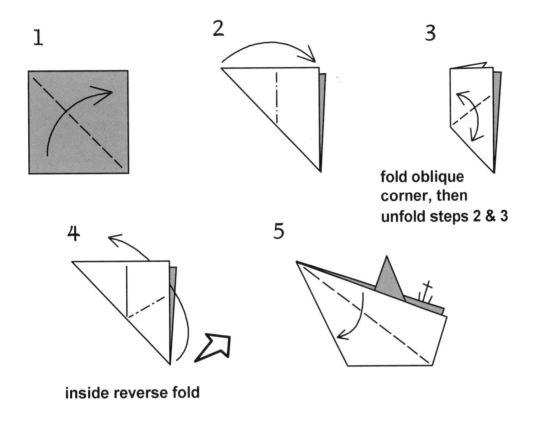

1

2

3

fold oblique
corner, then
unfold steps 2 & 3

4

inside reverse fold

5

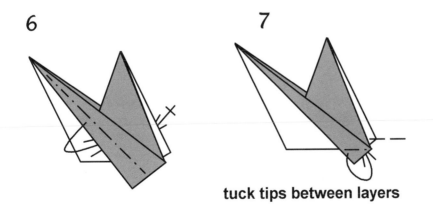

6

7

tuck tips between layers

this is the finished unit

the instructions for each model
will tell you how many units
to make

CELTIC BROOCH 11

Use Celtic Brooch Unit 3 page 19   make 10 units

A

Assembly

insert tips into pockets
marked points meet

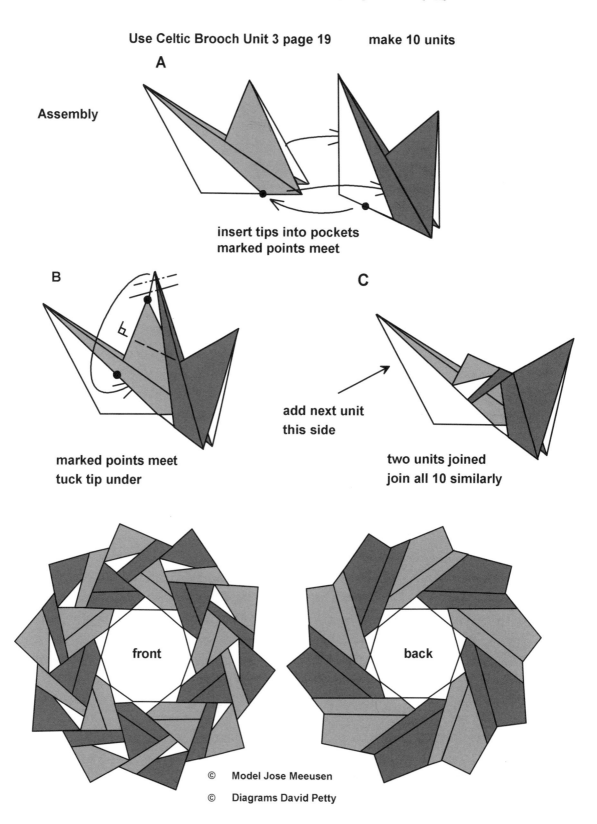

B

marked points meet
tuck tip under

C

add next unit
this side

two units joined
join all 10 similarly

front

back

©   Model Jose Meeusen

©   Diagrams David Petty

1: CELTIC BROOCHES   20

CELTIC BROOCH 12

Use Celtic Brooch Unit 3 page 19   **make 10 units**

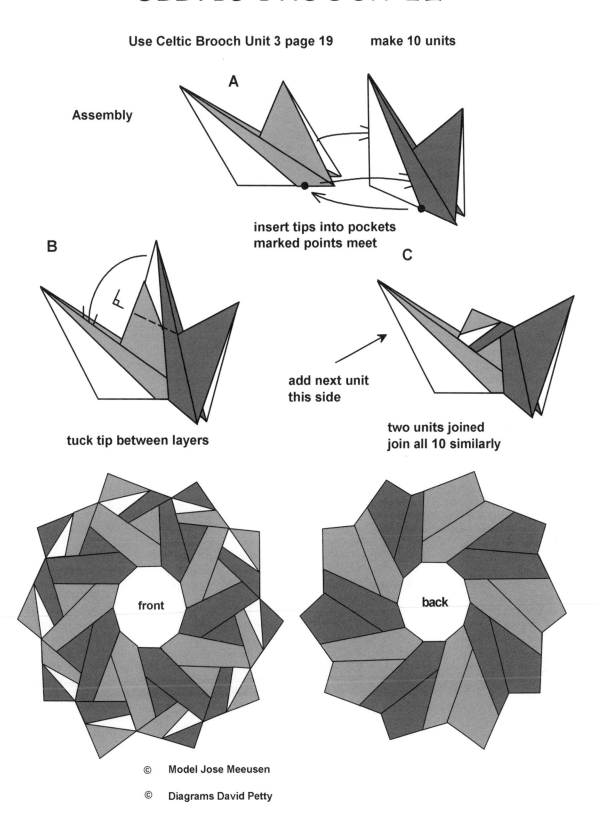

Assembly

A

insert tips into pockets
marked points meet

B

tuck tip between layers

C

add next unit
this side

two units joined
join all 10 similarly

front

back

© Model Jose Meeusen

© Diagrams David Petty

CELTIC BROOCH 13

Use Celtic Brooch Unit 3 page 19   make 10 units

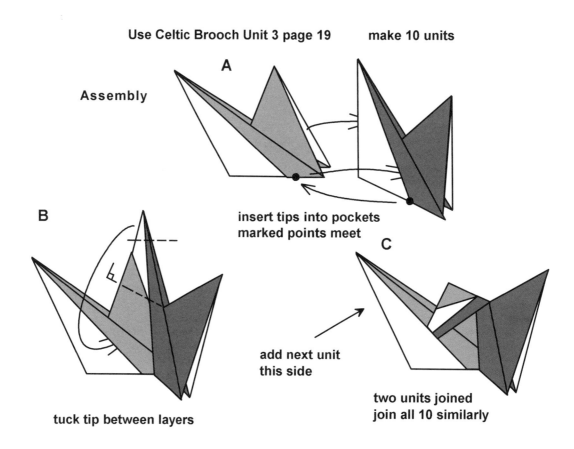

A

Assembly

insert tips into pockets
marked points meet

B

tuck tip between layers

add next unit
this side

C

two units joined
join all 10 similarly

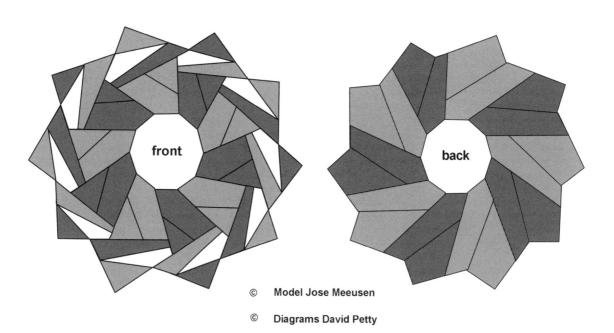

front

back

©   Model Jose Meeusen

©   Diagrams David Petty

CELTIC BROOCH 14

Use Celtic Brooch Unit 3 page 19   make 12 units

A

Assembly

insert tips into pockets
marked points meet

B

tuck tip into pocket

marked points meet

C

add next unit
this side

two units joined
join all 12 similarly

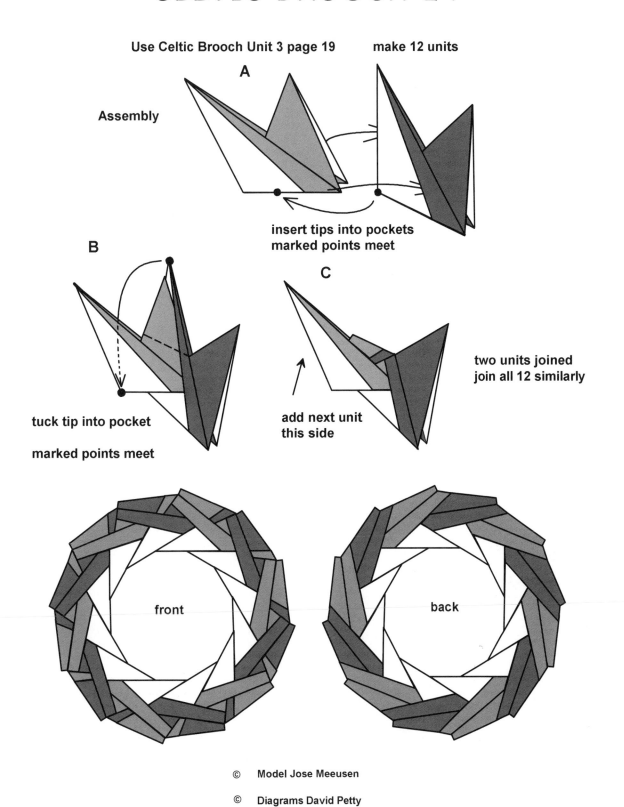

front

back

©   **Model Jose Meeusen**

©   **Diagrams David Petty**

1: CELTIC BROOCHES

CELTIC BROOCH 15

Use Celtic Brooch Unit 3 page 19   make 12 units

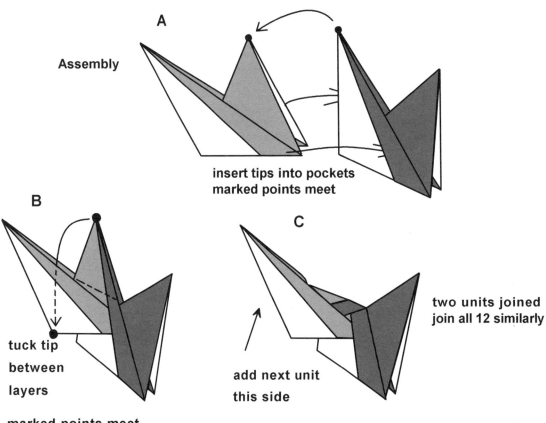

A

Assembly

insert tips into pockets
marked points meet

B

tuck tip
between
layers

marked points meet

C

add next unit
this side

two units joined
join all 12 similarly

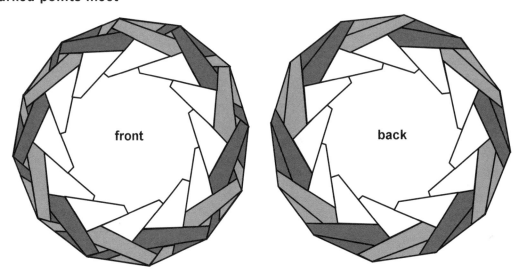

front

back

© Model Jose Meeusen

© Diagrams David Petty

CELTIC BROOCH 16

Use Celtic Brooch Unit 3 page 19   make 12 units

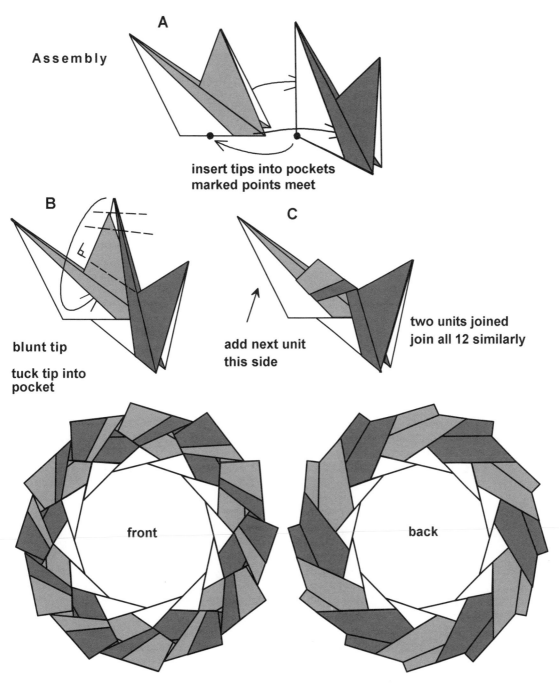

A

Assembly

insert tips into pockets
marked points meet

B

blunt tip

tuck tip into
pocket

C

add next unit
this side

two units joined
join all 12 similarly

front

back

© Model Jose Meeusen

© Diagrams David Petty

CELTIC BROOCH 17

Use Celtic Brooch Unit 3 page 19   make 12 units

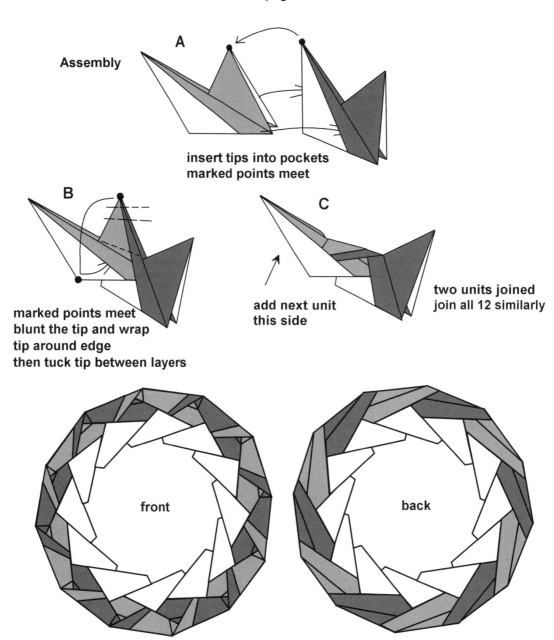

Assembly

A

insert tips into pockets
marked points meet

B

marked points meet
blunt the tip and wrap
tip around edge
then tuck tip between layers

C

add next unit
this side

two units joined
join all 12 similarly

front

back

© Model Jose Meeusen

© Diagrams David Petty

1: CELTIC BROOCHES   26

CELTIC BROOCH UNIT 4

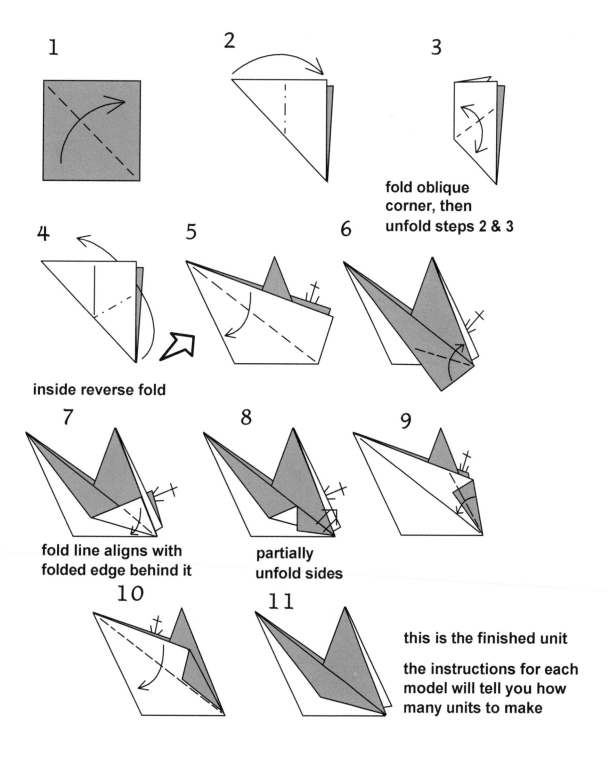

1

2

3

fold oblique
corner, then
unfold steps 2 & 3

4

inside reverse fold

5

6

7

fold line aligns with
folded edge behind it

8

partially
unfold sides

9

10

11

this is the finished unit

the instructions for each
model will tell you how
many units to make

CELTIC BROOCH 18

Use Celtic Brooch Unit 4 page 27   make 12 units

Assembly

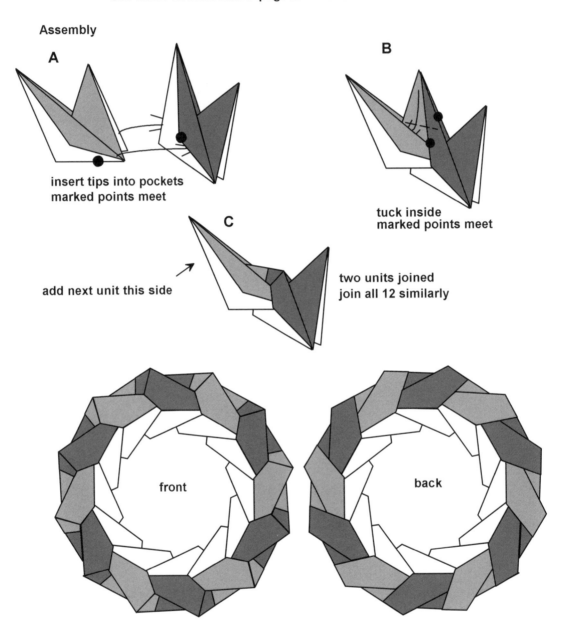

A

insert tips into pockets
marked points meet

B

tuck inside
marked points meet

C

add next unit this side

two units joined
join all 12 similarly

front

back

©   **Model David Petty**

©   **Diagrams David Petty**

CELTIC BROOCH 19

Use Celtic Brooch Unit 4 page 27   make 12 units

Assembly

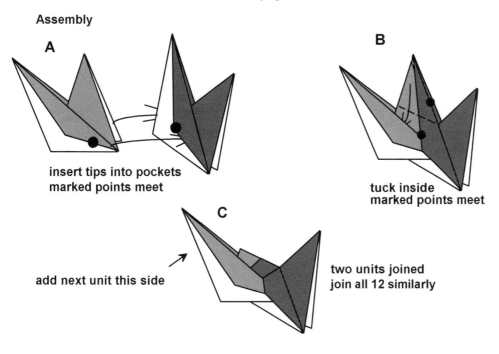

A

insert tips into pockets
marked points meet

B

tuck inside
marked points meet

C

add next unit this side

two units joined
join all 12 similarly

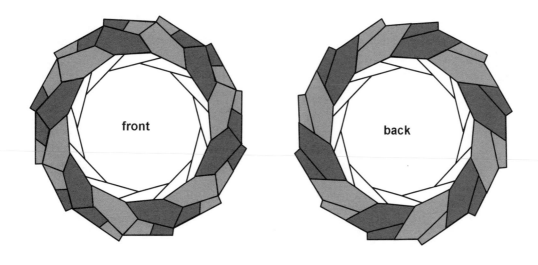

front

back

©   Model David Petty

©   Diagrams David Petty

CELTIC BROOCH 20

Use Celtic Brooch Unit 4 page 27   make 11 units

Assembly

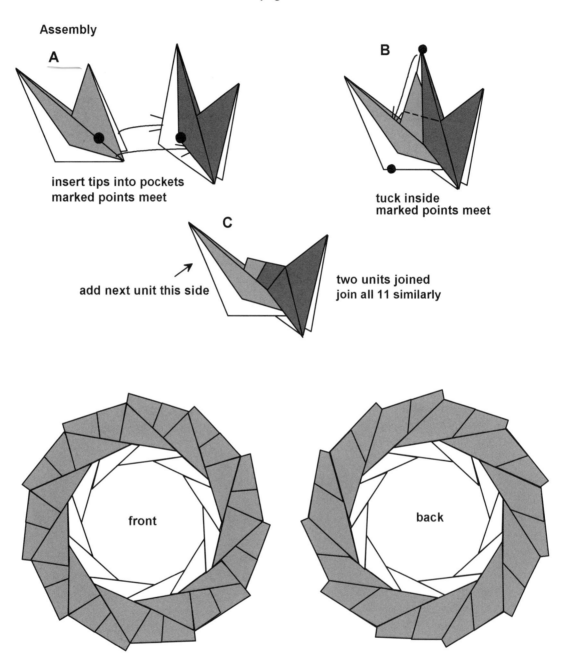

A

insert tips into pockets
marked points meet

B

tuck inside
marked points meet

C

add next unit this side

two units joined
join all 11 similarly

front

back

© **Model David Petty**

© **Diagrams David Petty**

CELTIC BROOCH UNIT 5

1

2

3

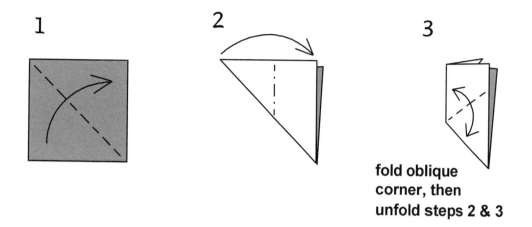

fold oblique
corner, then
unfold steps 2 & 3

4

5

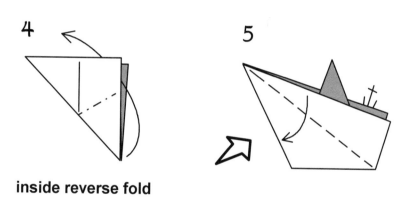

inside reverse fold

6

7

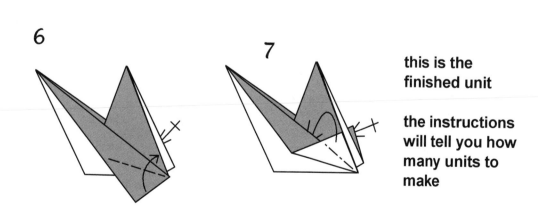

this is the
finished unit

the instructions
will tell you how
many units to
make

CELTIC BROOCH 21

Use Celtic Brooch Unit 5 page 31   **make 12 units**

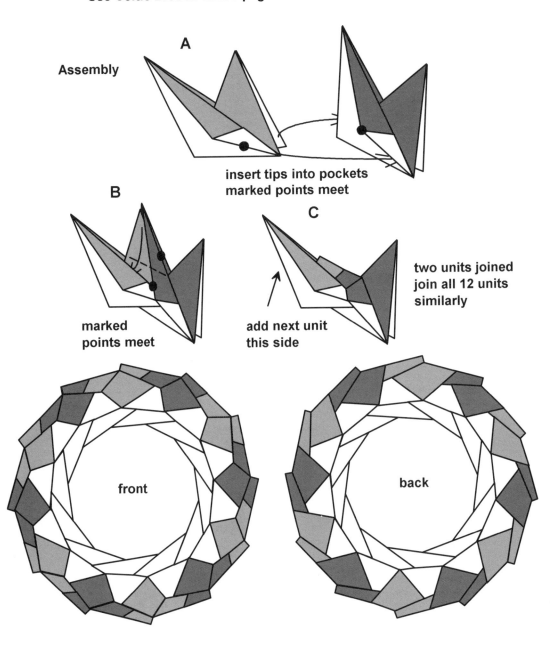

A

Assembly

insert tips into pockets
marked points meet

B

marked
points meet

C

add next unit
this side

two units joined
join all 12 units
similarly

front

back

©   **Model David Petty**

©   **Diagrams David Petty**

CELTIC BROOCH 22

Use Celtic Brooch Unit 5 page 31 **make 10 units**

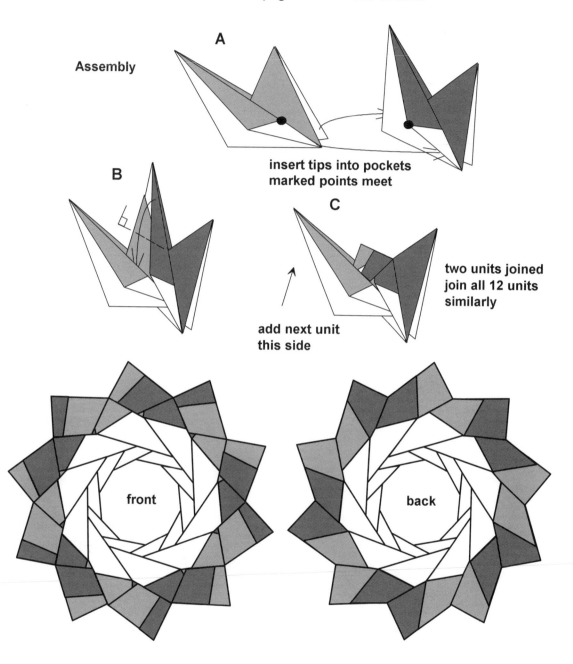

Assembly

A

insert tips into pockets
marked points meet

B

C

two units joined
join all 12 units
similarly

add next unit
this side

front

back

©   Model David Petty

©   Diagrams David Petty

CELTIC BROOCH UNIT 6

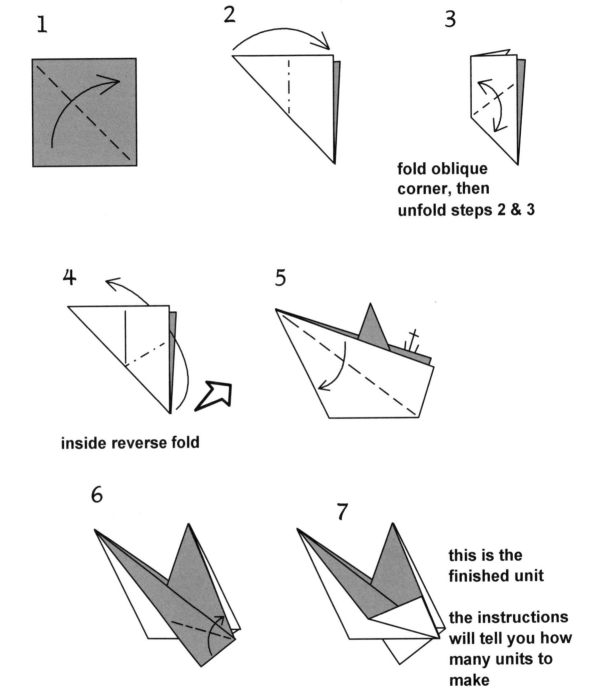

1

2

3

fold oblique
corner, then
unfold steps 2 & 3

4

inside reverse fold

5

6

7

this is the
finished unit

the instructions
will tell you how
many units to
make

CELTIC BROOCH 23

Use Celtic Brooch Unit 6 page 34   make 10 units

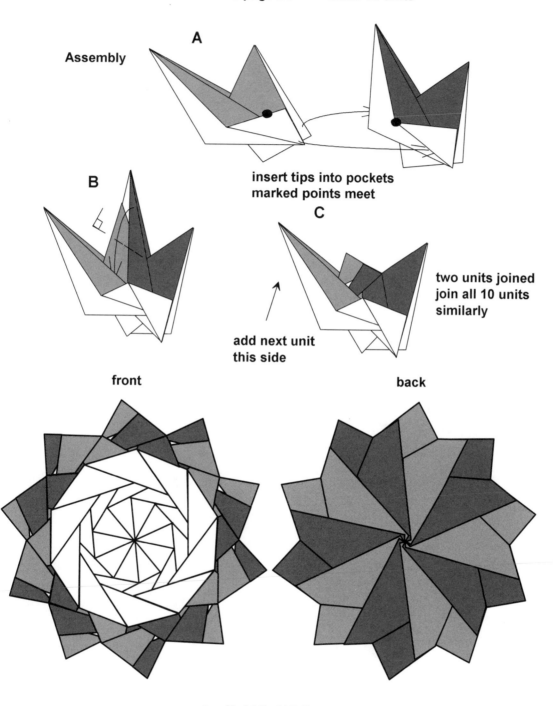

Assembly

A

B

insert tips into pockets
marked points meet

C

add next unit
this side

two units joined
join all 10 units
similarly

front   back

© Model David Petty

© Diagrams David Petty

CELTIC GARLAND 1

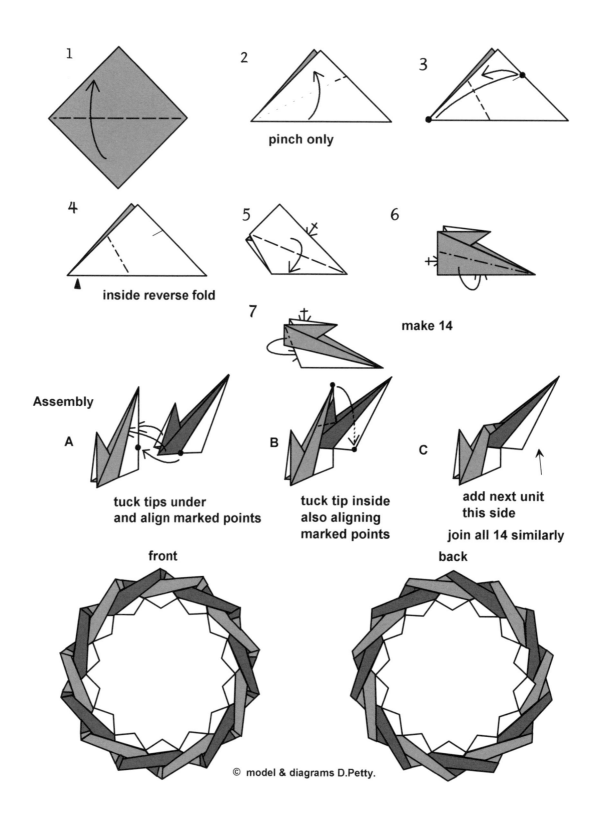

1

2

pinch only

3

4

inside reverse fold

5

6

7

make 14

Assembly

A

tuck tips under
and align marked points

B

tuck tip inside
also aligning
marked points

C

add next unit
this side

join all 14 similarly

front

back

© model & diagrams D.Petty.

CELTIC GARLAND 2

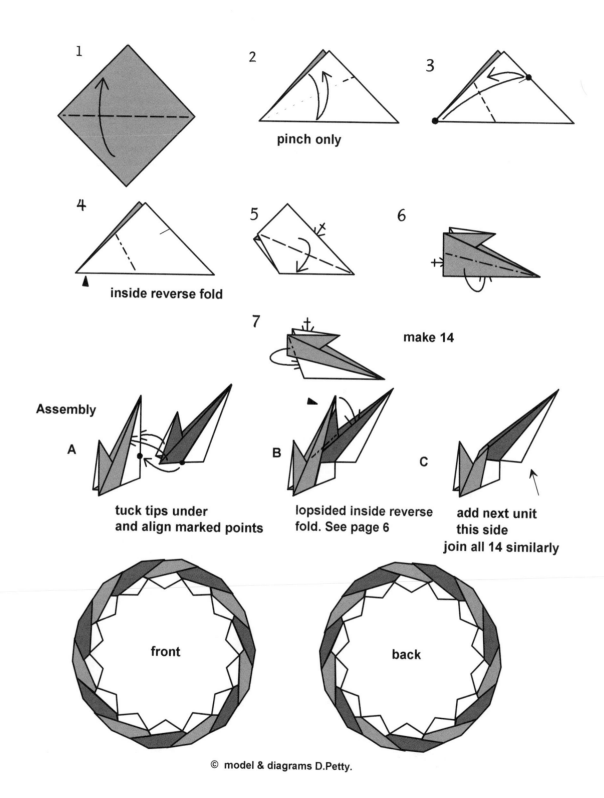

1

2

pinch only

3

4

inside reverse fold

5

6

7

make 14

Assembly

A

tuck tips under
and align marked points

B

lopsided inside reverse
fold. See page 6

C

add next unit
this side
join all 14 similarly

front

back

© model & diagrams D.Petty.

2: CELTIC GARLANDS

CELTIC GARLAND 3

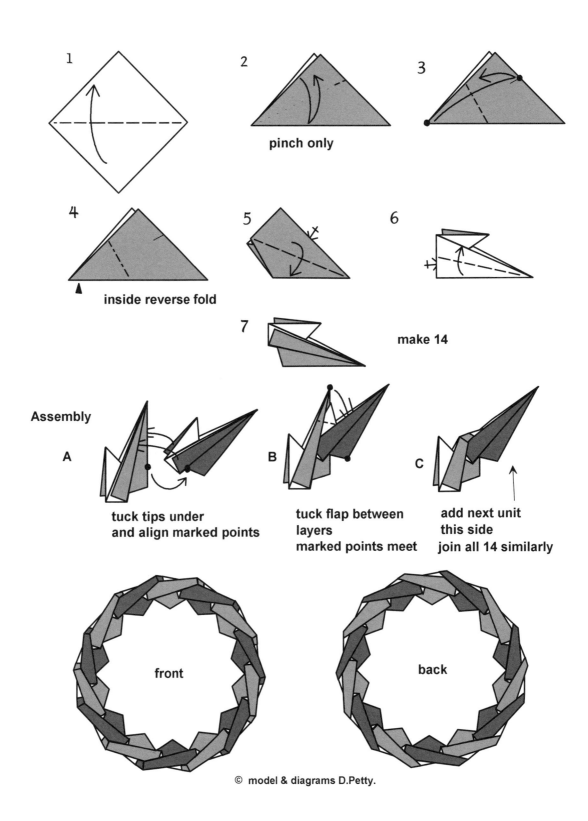

1

2
pinch only

3

4
inside reverse fold

5

6

7
make 14

Assembly

A
tuck tips under
and align marked points

B
tuck flap between
layers
marked points meet

C
add next unit
this side
join all 14 similarly

front

back

© model & diagrams D.Petty.

CELTIC GARLAND 4

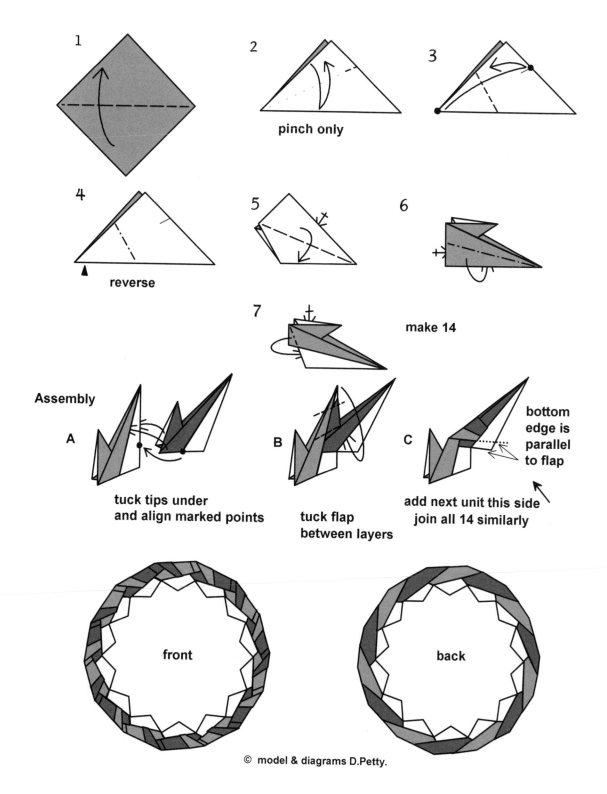

1

2 pinch only

3

4 reverse

5

6

7 make 14

Assembly

A tuck tips under and align marked points

B tuck flap between layers

C add next unit this side join all 14 similarly

bottom edge is parallel to flap

front

back

© model & diagrams D.Petty.

CELTIC MOTIF 1

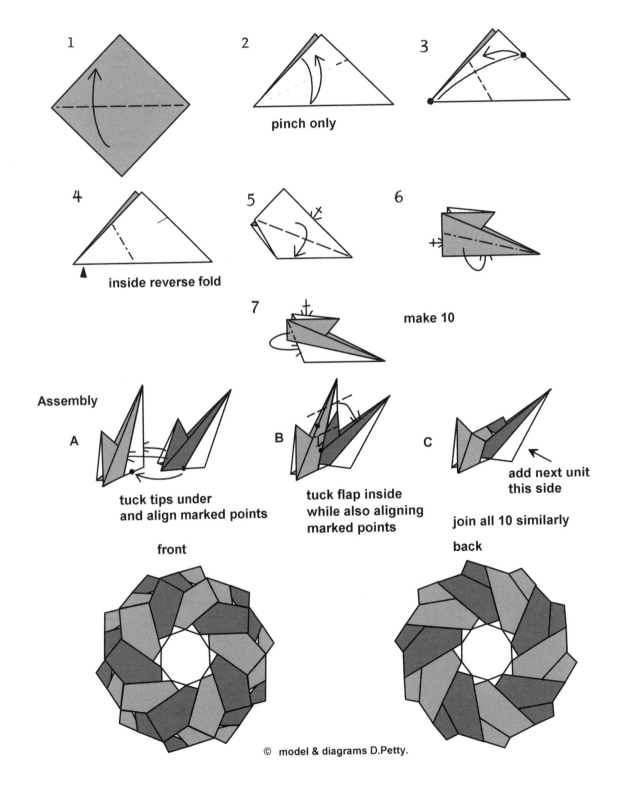

1

2

pinch only

3

4

inside reverse fold

5

6

7

make 10

Assembly

A

tuck tips under
and align marked points

B

tuck flap inside
while also aligning
marked points

C

add next unit
this side

join all 10 similarly

front

back

© model & diagrams D.Petty.

CELTIC MOTIF 2

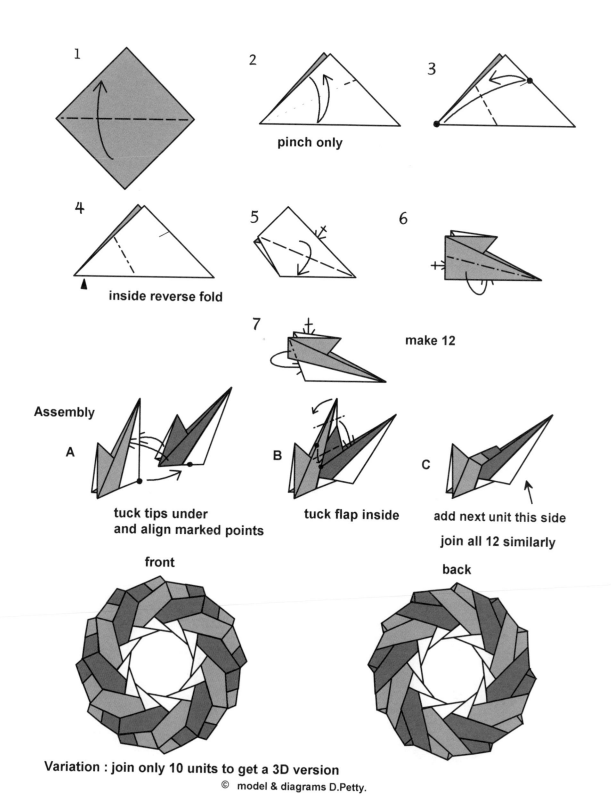

1

2

pinch only

3

4

inside reverse fold

5

6

7

make 12

Assembly

A

tuck tips under
and align marked points

B

tuck flap inside

C

add next unit this side

join all 12 similarly

front

back

Variation : join only 10 units to get a 3D version

© model & diagrams D.Petty.

CELTIC MOTIF 3

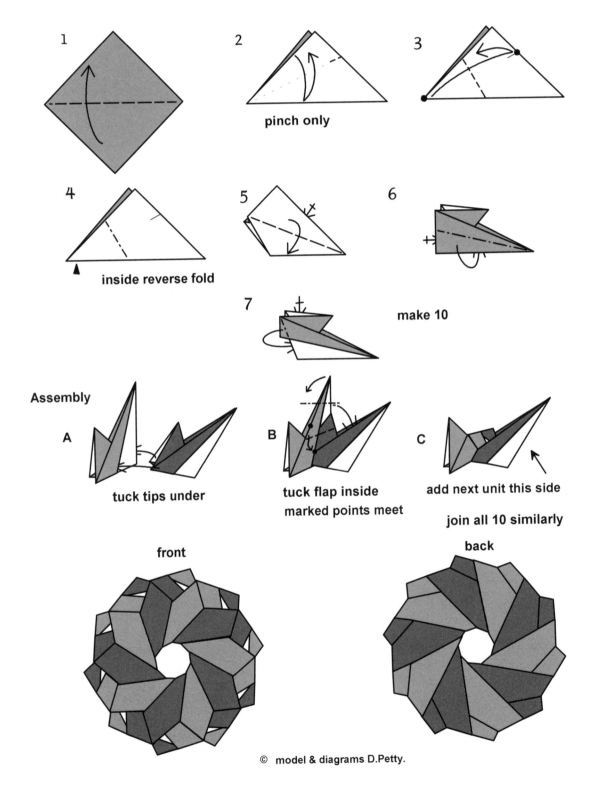

1

2 pinch only

3

4 inside reverse fold

5

6

7 make 10

Assembly

A tuck tips under

B tuck flap inside
marked points meet

C add next unit this side

join all 10 similarly

front

back

© model & diagrams D.Petty.

CELTIC MOTIF 4

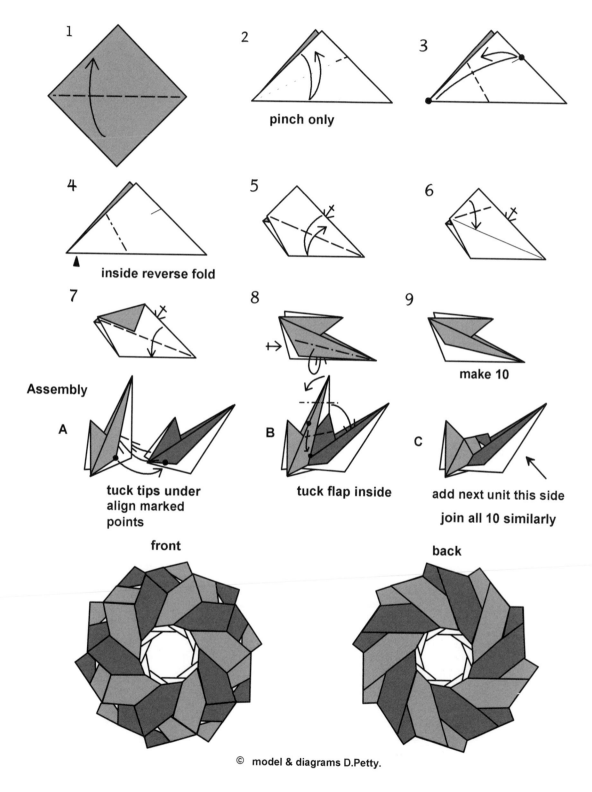

1

2 pinch only

3

4 inside reverse fold

5

6

7

8

9 make 10

Assembly

A tuck tips under
align marked
points

B tuck flap inside

C add next unit this side
join all 10 similarly

front

back

© model & diagrams D.Petty.

3: CELTIC MOTIFS

CELTIC MOTIF 5

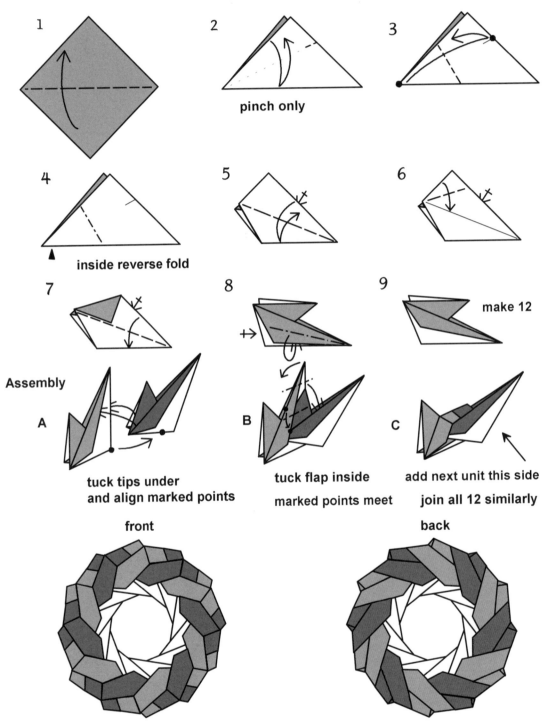

1

2

pinch only

3

4

inside reverse fold

5

6

7

8

9

make 12

Assembly

A

tuck tips under
and align marked points

B

tuck flap inside

marked points meet

C

add next unit this side

join all 12 similarly

front

back

Variation : join only 10 units to get a 3D version

© model & diagrams D.Petty.

CELTIC MOTIF 6

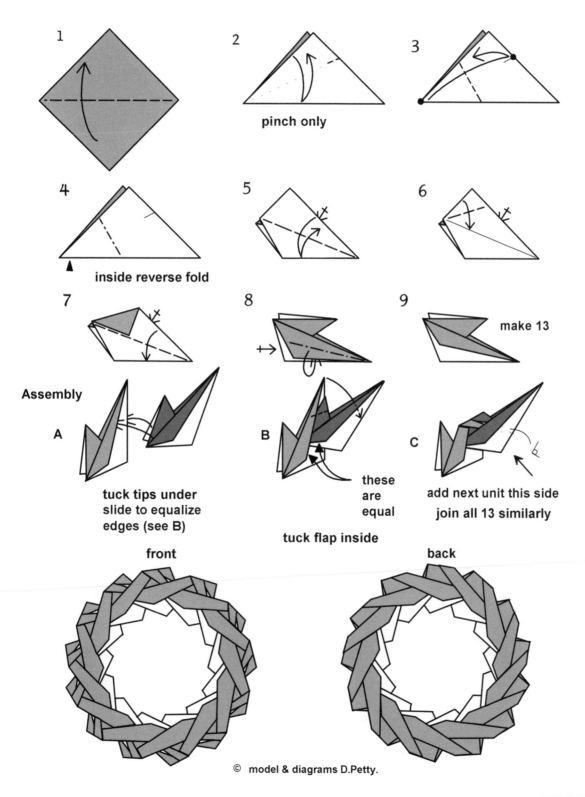

1

2 **pinch only**

3

4 **inside reverse fold**

5

6

7

8 **these are equal**

9 **make 13**

Assembly

A **tuck tips under slide to equalize edges (see B)**

B **tuck flap inside**

C **add next unit this side join all 13 similarly**

front

back

© model & diagrams D.Petty.

CELTIC MOTIF 7

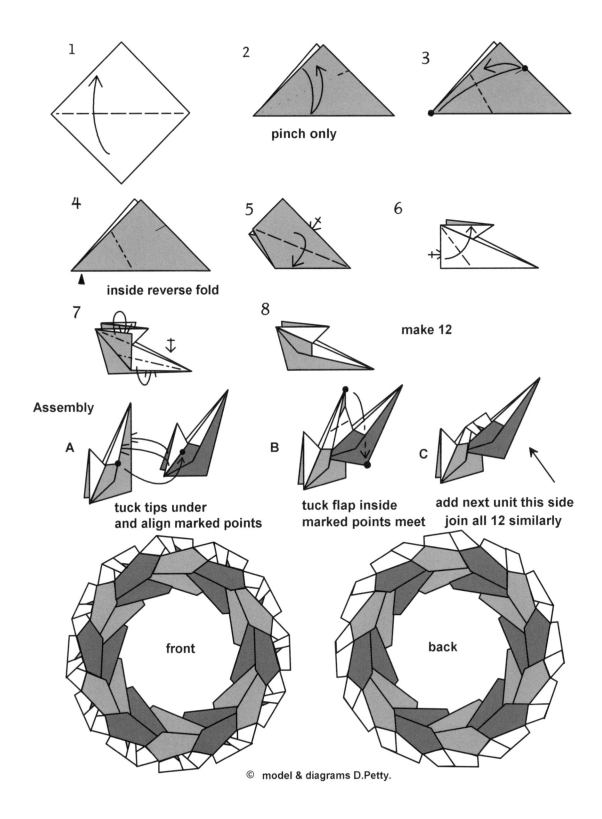

1

2

pinch only

3

4

inside reverse fold

5

6

7

8

make 12

Assembly

A

tuck tips under
and align marked points

B

tuck flap inside
marked points meet

C

add next unit this side
join all 12 similarly

front

back

© model & diagrams D.Petty.

CELTIC MOTIF 8

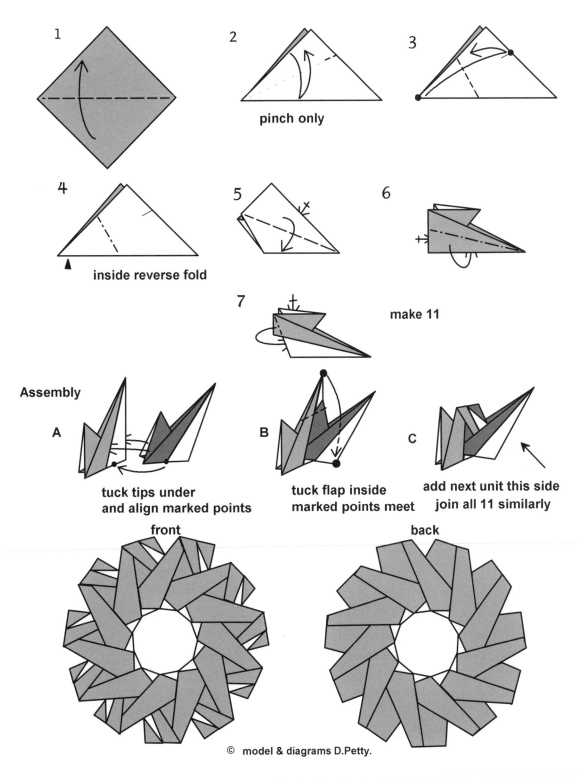

1

2

pinch only

3

4

inside reverse fold

5

6

7

make 11

Assembly

A

tuck tips under
and align marked points

B

tuck flap inside
marked points meet

C

add next unit this side
join all 11 similarly

front

back

© model & diagrams D.Petty.

CELTIC MOTIF 9

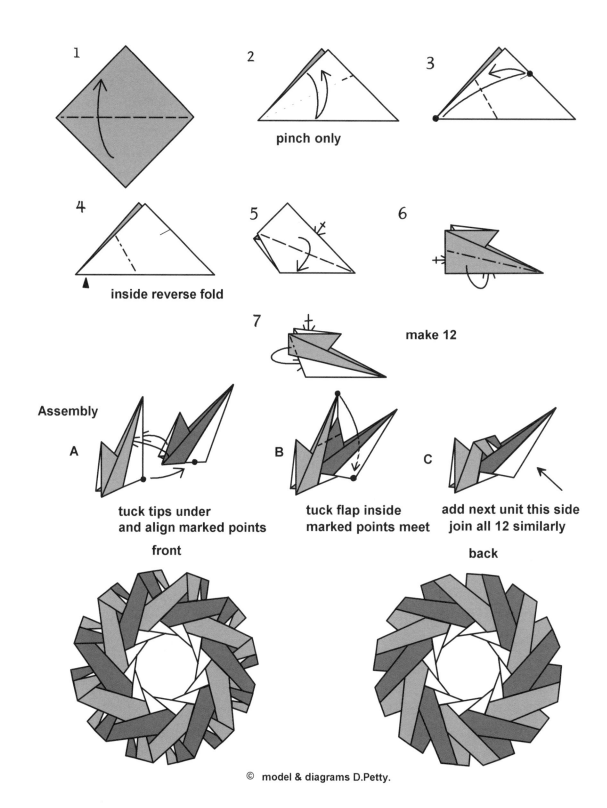

1

2

pinch only

3

4

inside reverse fold

5

6

7

make 12

Assembly

A

tuck tips under
and align marked points

front

B

tuck flap inside
marked points meet

back

C

add next unit this side
join all 12 similarly

© model & diagrams D.Petty.

CELTIC MOTIF 10

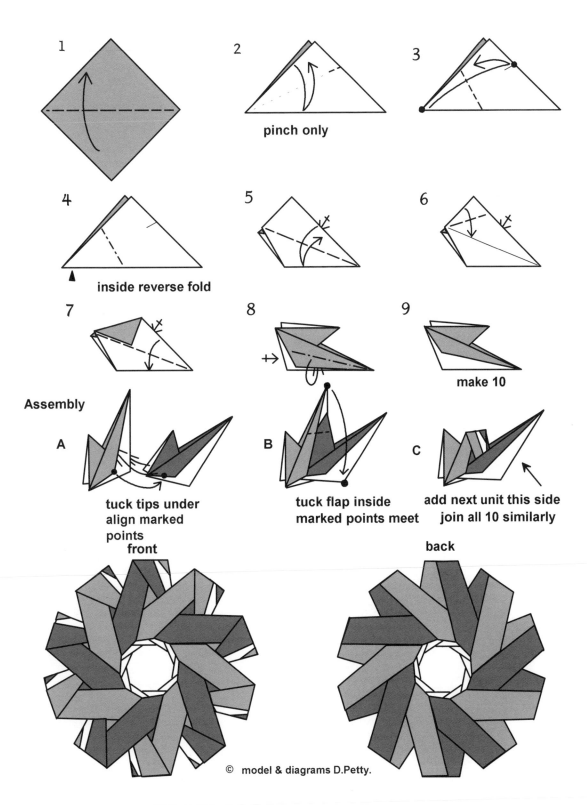

1

2

pinch only

3

4

inside reverse fold

5

6

7

8

9

make 10

Assembly

A

tuck tips under
align marked
points
front

B

tuck flap inside
marked points meet

C

add next unit this side
join all 10 similarly

back

© model & diagrams D.Petty.

CELTIC MOTIF 11

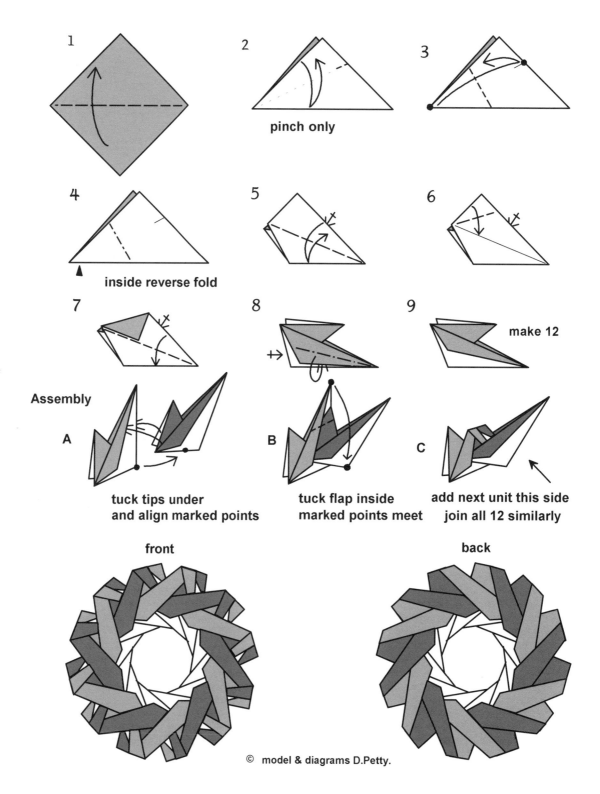

1

2

pinch only

3

4

inside reverse fold

5

6

7

8

9

make 12

Assembly

A

tuck tips under
and align marked points

B

tuck flap inside
marked points meet

C

add next unit this side
join all 12 similarly

front

back

© model & diagrams D.Petty.

CELTIC MOTIF 12

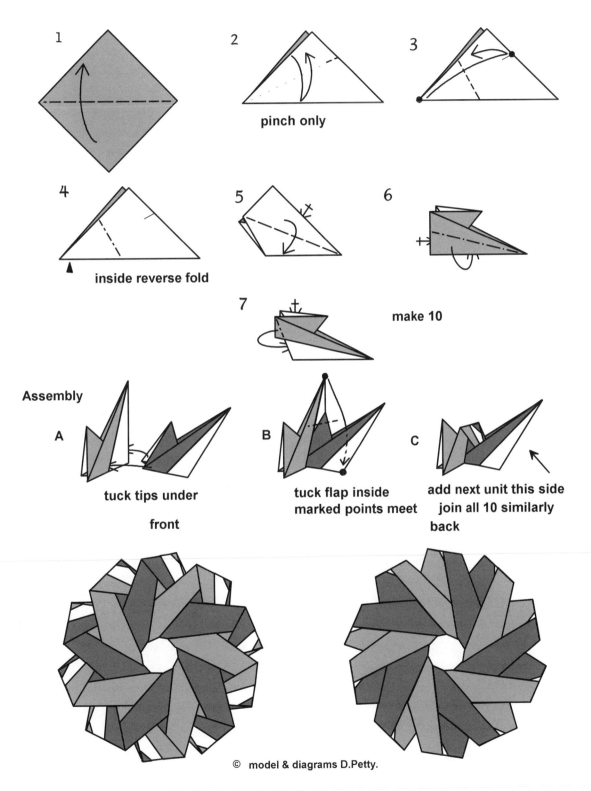

1

2

pinch only

3

4

inside reverse fold

5

6

7

make 10

Assembly

A

tuck tips under

front

B

tuck flap inside
marked points meet

C

add next unit this side
join all 10 similarly

back

© model & diagrams D.Petty.

3: CELTIC MOTIFS

CELTIC MOTIF 13

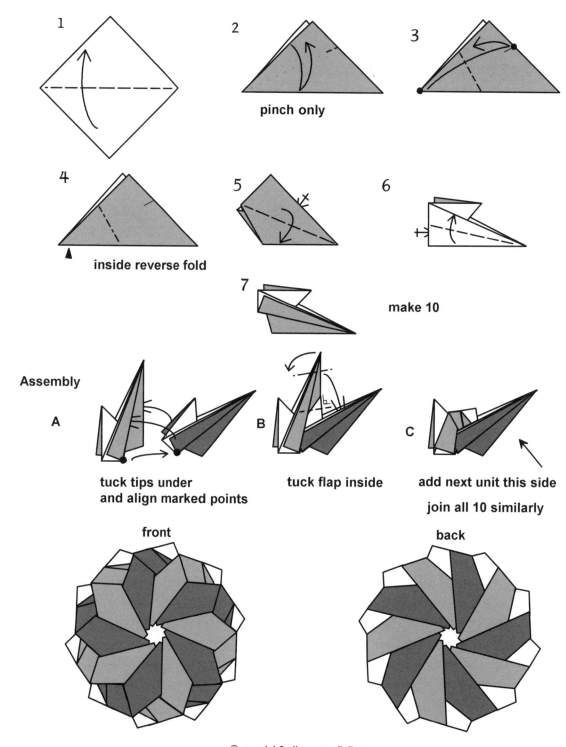

1

2

pinch only

3

4

inside reverse fold

5

6

7

make 10

Assembly

A

tuck tips under
and align marked points

B

tuck flap inside

C

add next unit this side

join all 10 similarly

front

back

© model & diagrams D.Petty.

CELTIC MOTIF 14

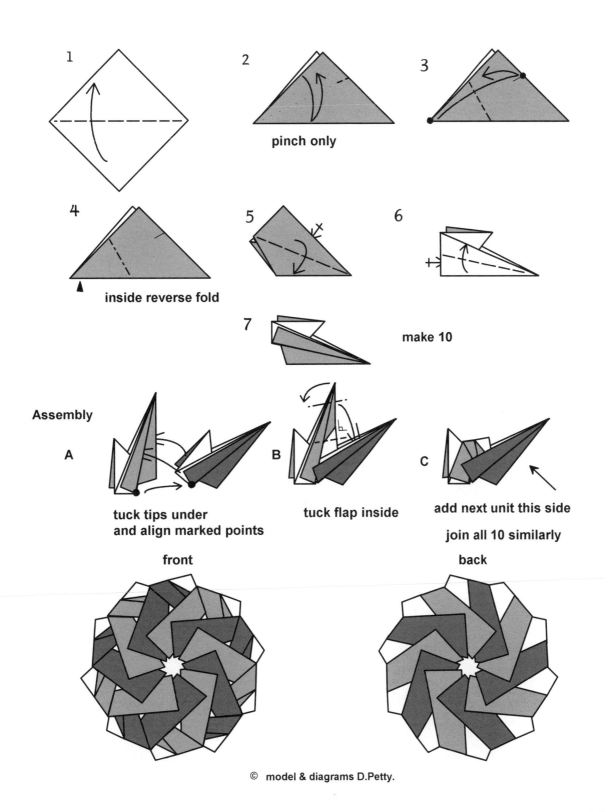

1

2

pinch only

3

4

▲ **inside reverse fold**

5

6

7

make 10

Assembly

A

**tuck tips under
and align marked points**

B

tuck flap inside

C

add next unit this side

join all 10 similarly

front

back

© model & diagrams D.Petty.

3: CELTIC MOTIFS

CELTIC MOTIF 15

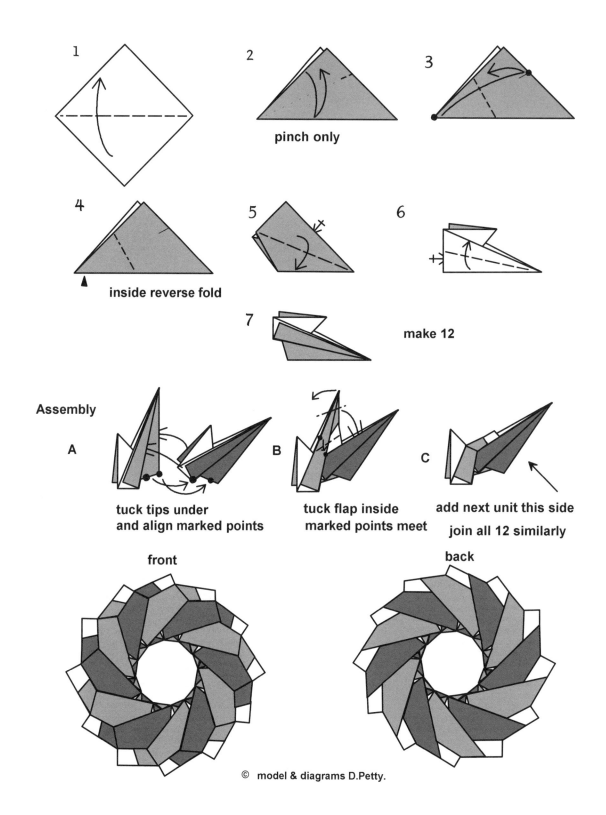

1

2

pinch only

3

4

▲ **inside reverse fold**

5

6

7

make 12

Assembly

A

**tuck tips under
and align marked points**

B

**tuck flap inside
marked points meet**

C

add next unit this side

join all 12 similarly

front

back

© model & diagrams D.Petty.

CELTIC MOTIF 16

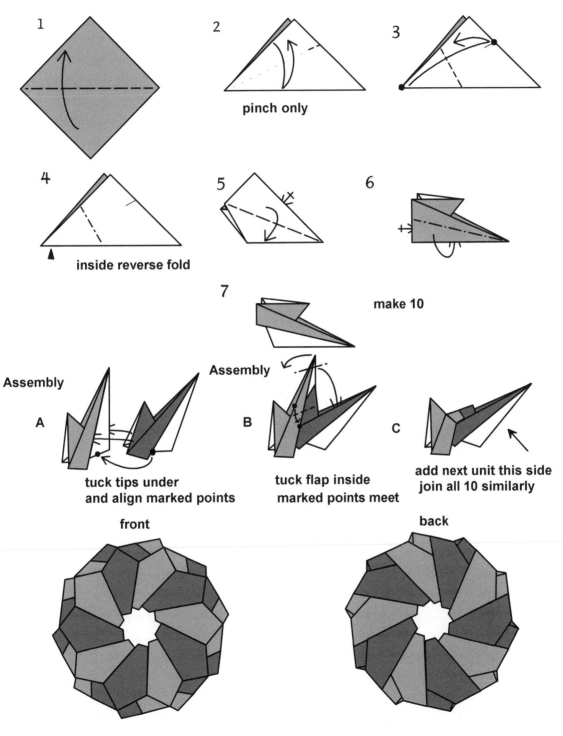

1

2

pinch only

3

4

inside reverse fold

5

6

7

make 10

Assembly

A

tuck tips under
and align marked points

Assembly

B

tuck flap inside
marked points meet

C

add next unit this side
join all 10 similarly

front

back

© model & diagrams D.Petty.

CELTIC MOTIF 17

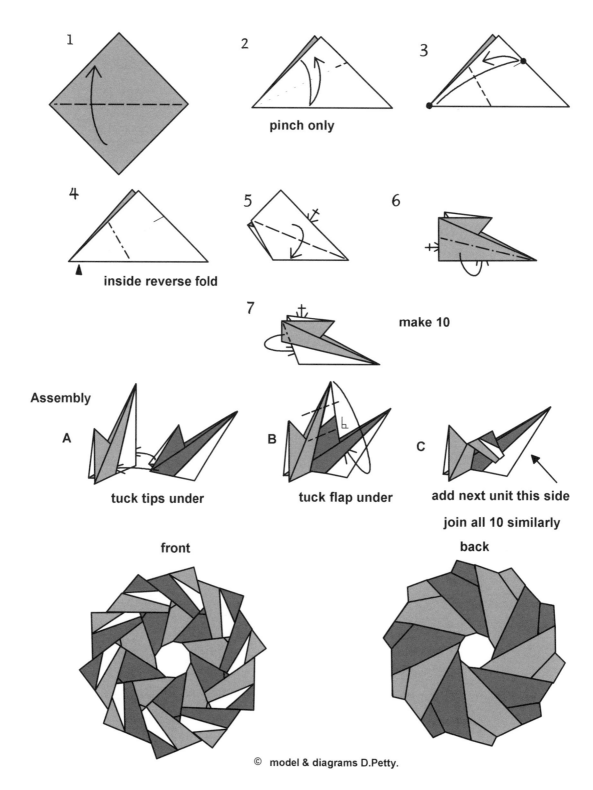

1

2

pinch only

3

4

inside reverse fold

5

6

7

make 10

Assembly

A

tuck tips under

B

tuck flap under

C

add next unit this side

join all 10 similarly

front

back

© model & diagrams D.Petty.

CELTIC MOTIF 18

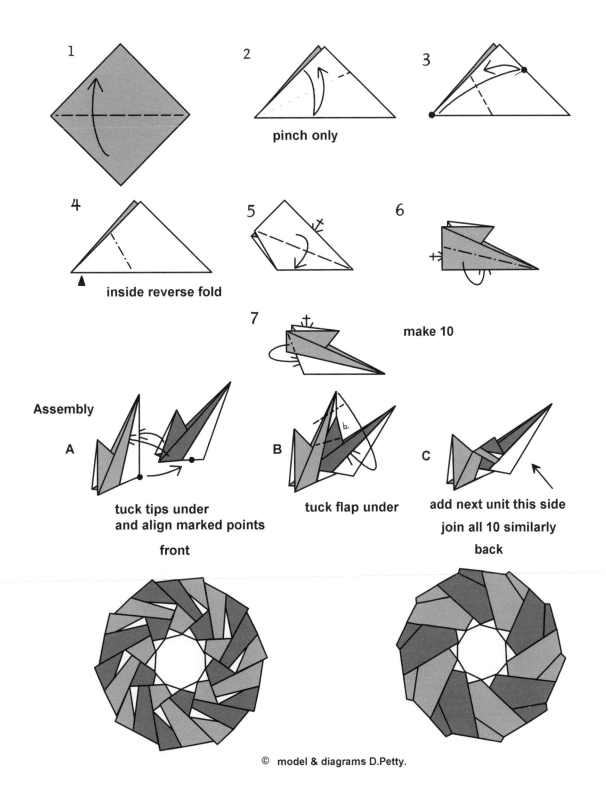

1

2

pinch only

3

4

inside reverse fold

5

6

7

make 10

Assembly

A

tuck tips under
and align marked points

front

B

tuck flap under

C

add next unit this side

join all 10 similarly

back

© model & diagrams D.Petty.

CELTIC MOTIF 19

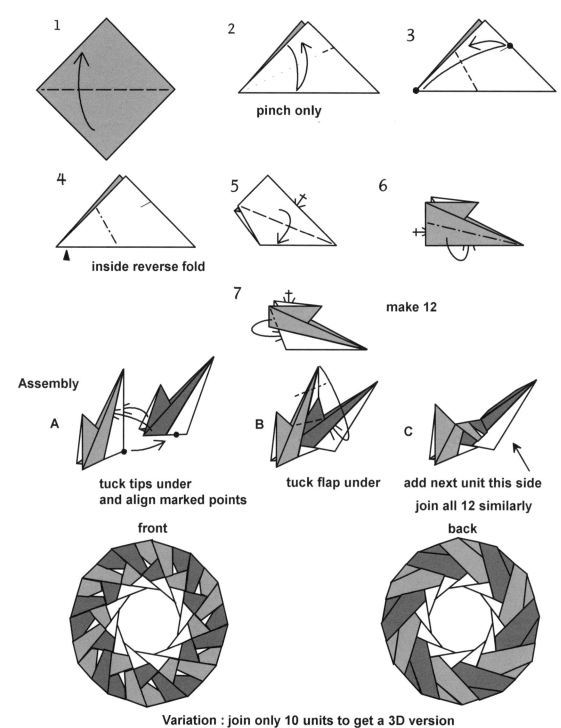

1

2

pinch only

3

4

inside reverse fold

5

6

7   make 12

Assembly

A

tuck tips under
and align marked points

B

tuck flap under

C

add next unit this side

join all 12 similarly

front

back

Variation : join only 10 units to get a 3D version

© model & diagrams D.Petty.

CELTIC MOTIF 20

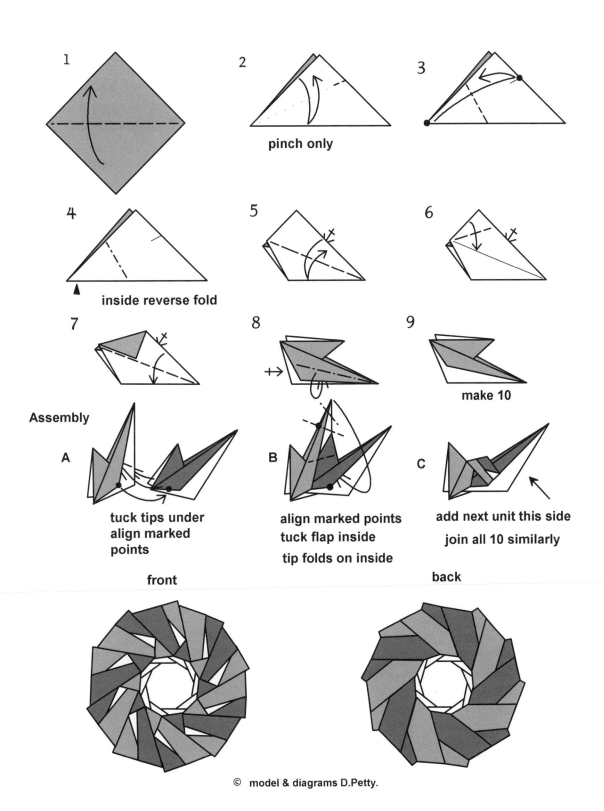

1

2
pinch only

3

4
inside reverse fold

5

6

7

8

9
make 10

Assembly

A
tuck tips under
align marked
points

front

B
align marked points
tuck flap inside
tip folds on inside

C
add next unit this side
join all 10 similarly

back

© model & diagrams D.Petty.

CELTIC MOTIF 21

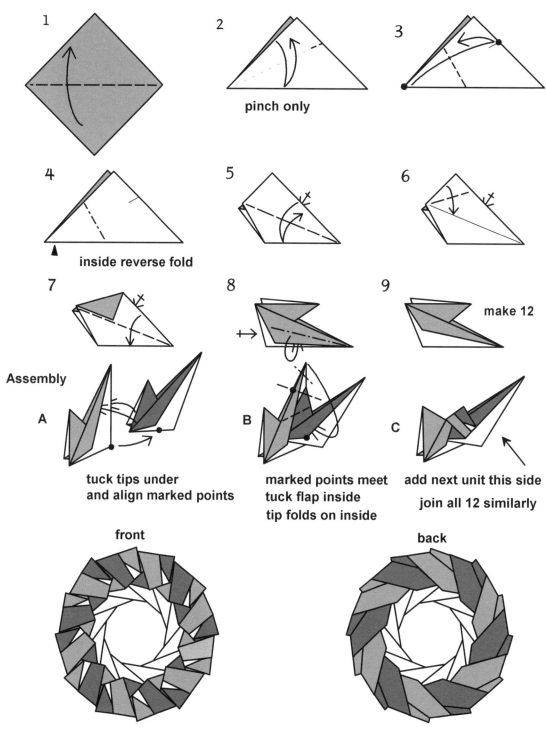

1

2

pinch only

3

4

inside reverse fold

5

6

7

8

9

make 12

Assembly

A

tuck tips under
and align marked points

B

marked points meet
tuck flap inside
tip folds on inside

C

add next unit this side

join all 12 similarly

front

back

Variation : join only 10 units to get a 3D version
© model & diagrams D.Petty.

CELTIC MOTIF 22

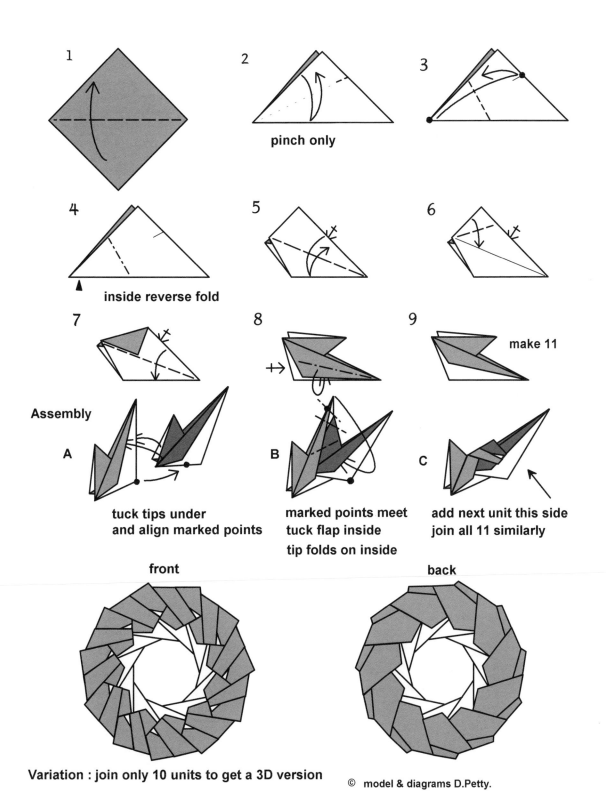

1

2 pinch only

3

4 inside reverse fold

5

6

7

8

9 make 11

Assembly

A tuck tips under and align marked points

B marked points meet
tuck flap inside
tip folds on inside

C add next unit this side
join all 11 similarly

front

back

Variation : join only 10 units to get a 3D version

© model & diagrams D.Petty.

CRANE WREATH UNIT 1

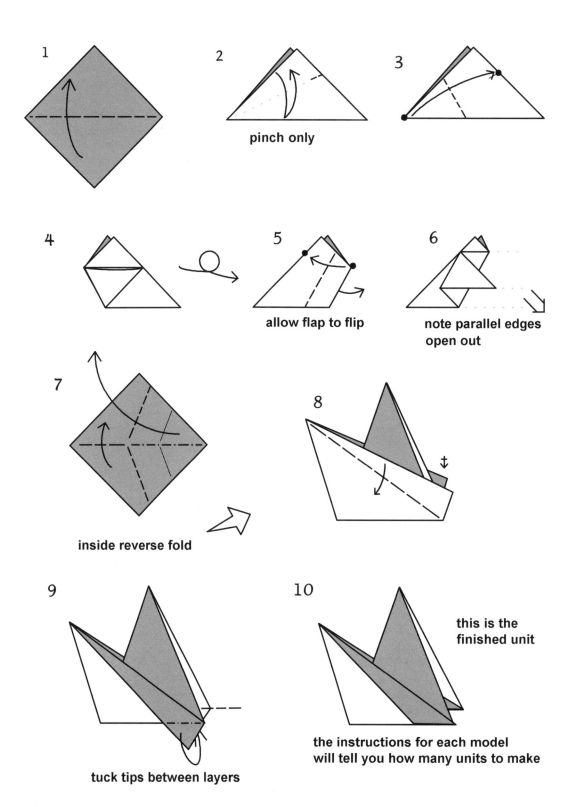

1

2

pinch only

3

4

allow flap to flip

5

6

**note parallel edges
open out**

7

inside reverse fold

8

9

tuck tips between layers

10

**this is the
finished unit**

**the instructions for each model
will tell you how many units to make**

CRANE WREATH 1

Use Crane Wreath Unit 1 page 62   make 10 units

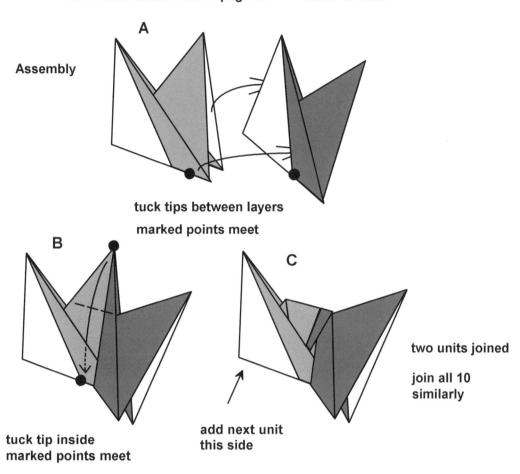

A

Assembly

tuck tips between layers

marked points meet

B

tuck tip inside
marked points meet

C

add next unit
this side

two units joined

join all 10
similarly

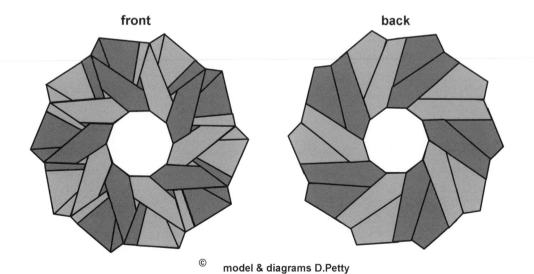

front

back

© model & diagrams D.Petty

CRANE WREATH 2

Use Crane Wreath Unit 1 page 62   make 10 units

A

Assembly

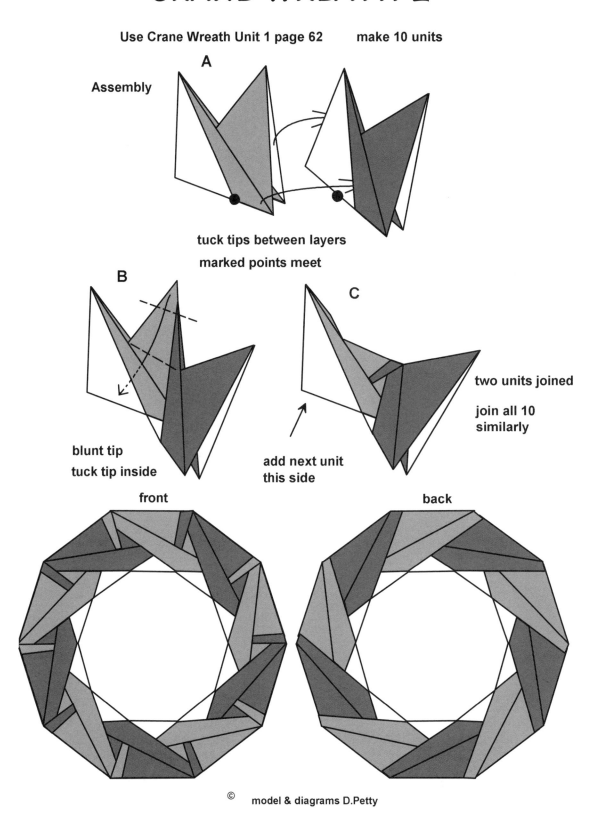

tuck tips between layers

marked points meet

B

blunt tip

tuck tip inside

C

two units joined

join all 10
similarly

add next unit
this side

front   back

© model & diagrams D.Petty

CRANE WREATH 3

Use Crane Wreath Unit 1 page 62   make 10 units

A

Assembly

tuck tips between layers

marked points meet

B

fold tip at
right angle
marked points meet
tuck tip inside

C

add next unit
this side

two units joined

join all 10
similarly

front

back

© model & diagrams D.Petty

CRANE WREATH 4

Use Crane Wreath Unit 1 page 62   make 10 units

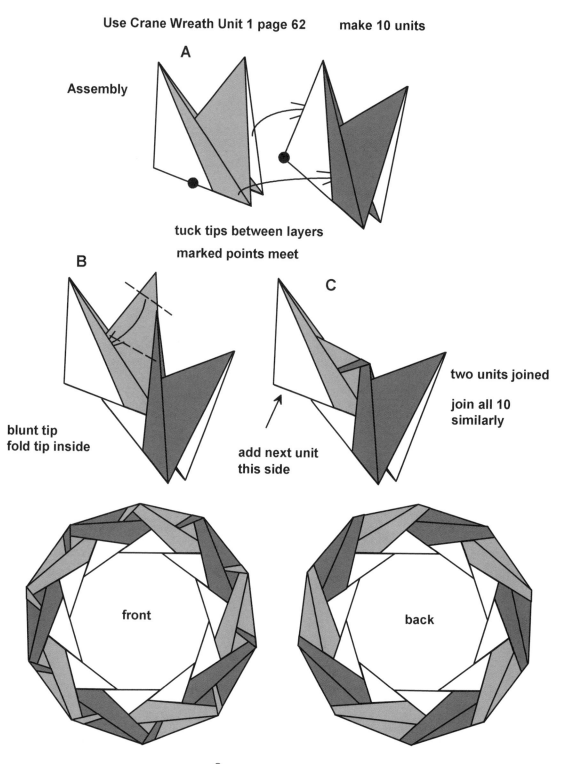

A

Assembly

tuck tips between layers

marked points meet

B

blunt tip
fold tip inside

C

two units joined

join all 10
similarly

add next unit
this side

front

back

© model & diagrams D.Petty

CRANE WREATH 5

Use Crane Wreath Unit 1 page 62

make 10 units

A

Assembly

tuck tips between layers

marked points meet

B

fold tip inside

marked points meet

C

two units joined

join all 10
similarly

add next unit
this side

front

back

© model & diagrams D.Petty

67

4: CRANE WREATHS

CRANE WREATH 6

Use Crane Wreath Unit 1 page 62   **make 10 units**

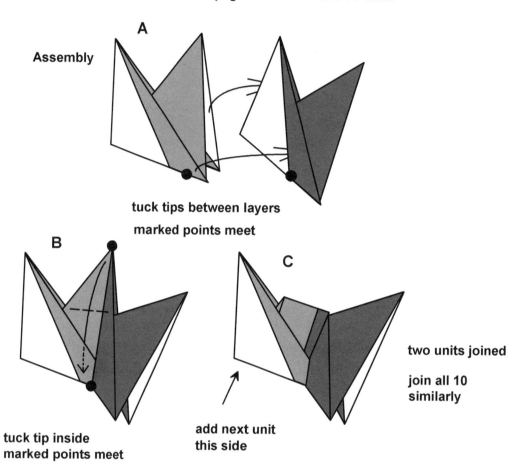

A

Assembly

tuck tips between layers

marked points meet

B

C

two units joined

join all 10
similarly

tuck tip inside
marked points meet

add next unit
this side

front   back

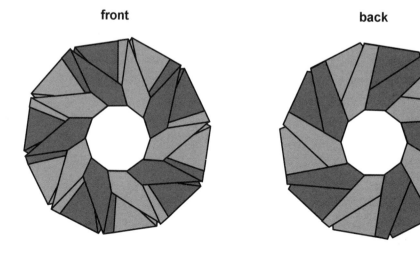

CRANE WREATH 7

Use Crane Wreath Unit 1 page 62   make 10 units

A

Assembly

tuck tips between layers

marked points meet

B

C

two units joined

join all 10
similarly

wrap around
edge and tuck
inside, blunting
tip

add next unit
this side

front   back

© model & diagrams D.Petty

CRANE WREATH UNIT 2

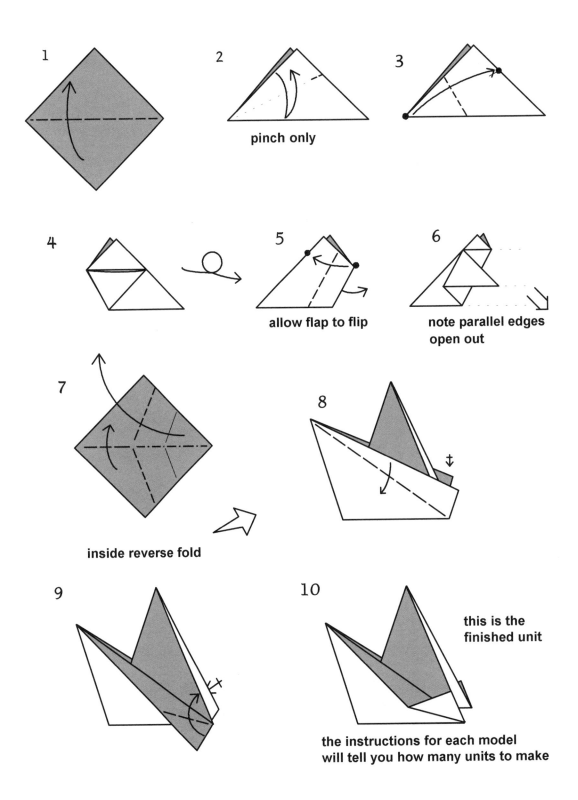

1

2

pinch only

3

4

5

allow flap to flip

6

note parallel edges
open out

7

inside reverse fold

8

9

10

this is the
finished unit

the instructions for each model
will tell you how many units to make

CRANE WREATH 8

Use Crane Wreath Unit 2 page 70   make 10 units

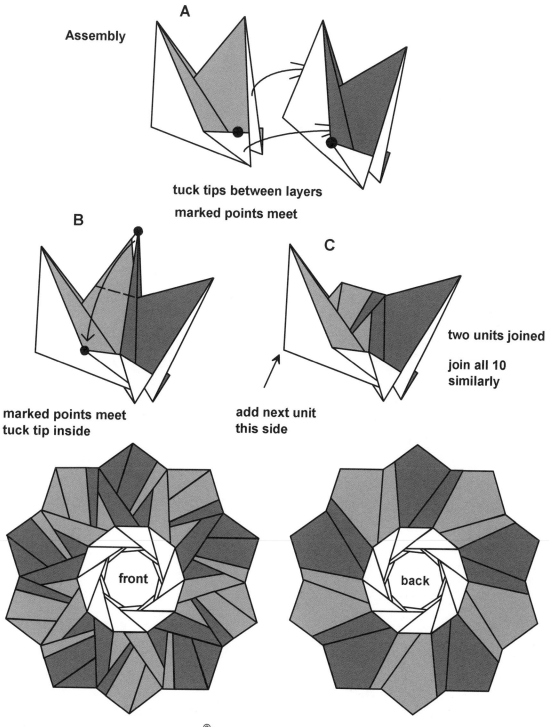

A

Assembly

tuck tips between layers

marked points meet

B

marked points meet
tuck tip inside

C

two units joined

join all 10
similarly

add next unit
this side

front

back

© model & diagrams D.Petty

4:CRANE WREATHS

CRANE WREATH 9

Use Crane Wreath Unit 2 page 70   make 10 units

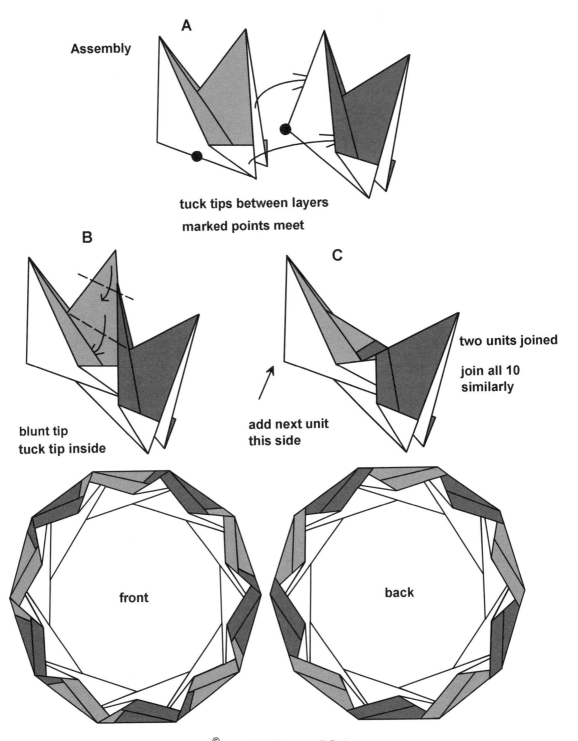

A

Assembly

tuck tips between layers

marked points meet

B

blunt tip
tuck tip inside

C

two units joined

join all 10
similarly

add next unit
this side

front

back

© model & diagrams D.Petty

CRANE WREATH 10

Use Crane Wreath Unit 2 page 70   make 10 units

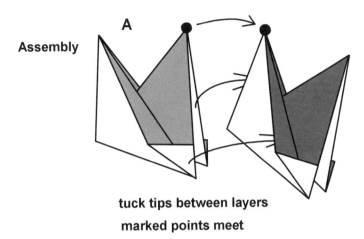

A

Assembly

tuck tips between layers

marked points meet

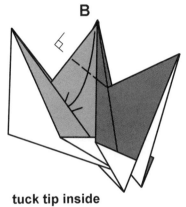

B

tuck tip inside

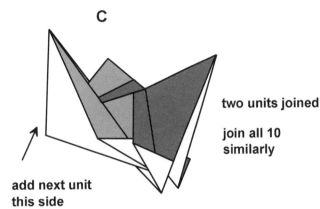

C

**add next unit
this side**

two units joined

**join all 10
similarly**

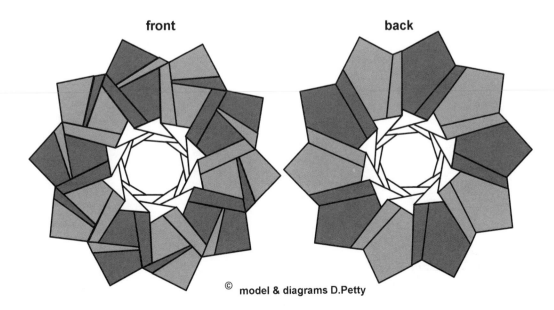

front   **back**

4: CRANE WREATHS

STAR GARLAND 1

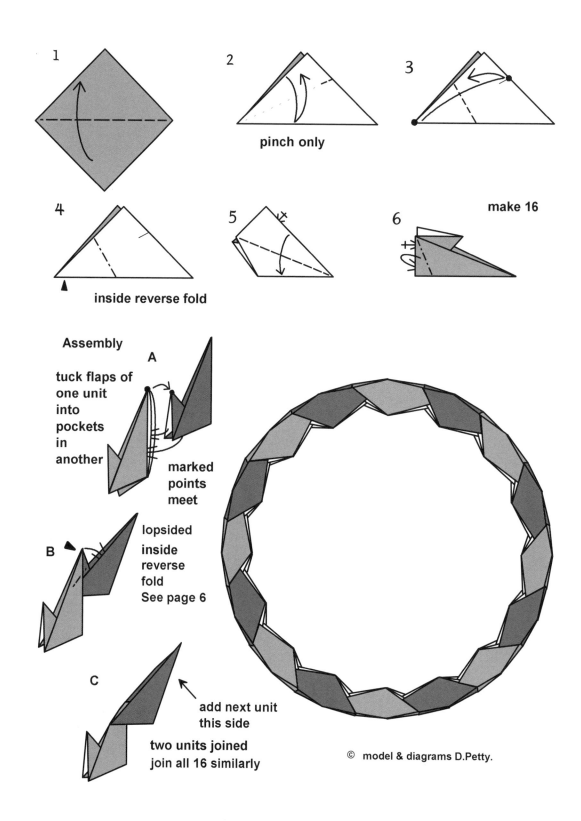

1

2 pinch only

3

4 inside reverse fold

5

6 make 16

Assembly

A
tuck flaps of
one unit
into
pockets
in
another

marked
points
meet

B
lopsided
inside
reverse
fold
See page 6

C
add next unit
this side

two units joined
join all 16 similarly

© model & diagrams D.Petty.

STAR GARLAND 2

1

2

pinch only

3

4

inside reverse fold

5

6

7

8

make 16

Assembly

A

tuck flaps of
one unit
into
pockets
in
another

marked points
meet

B

lopsided
inside
reverse
fold
See page 6

C

add next
unit this
side

two units joined
join all 16 similarly

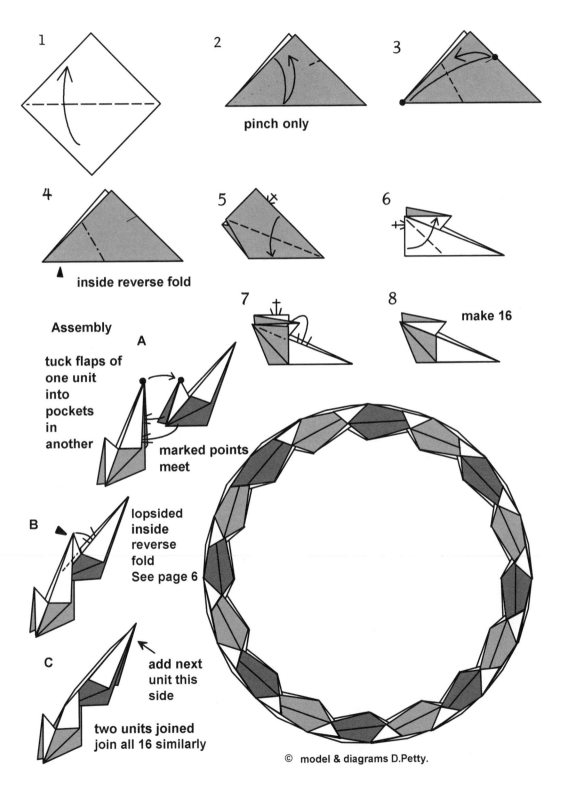

© model & diagrams D.Petty.

5: STAR GARLANDS

STAR GARLAND 3

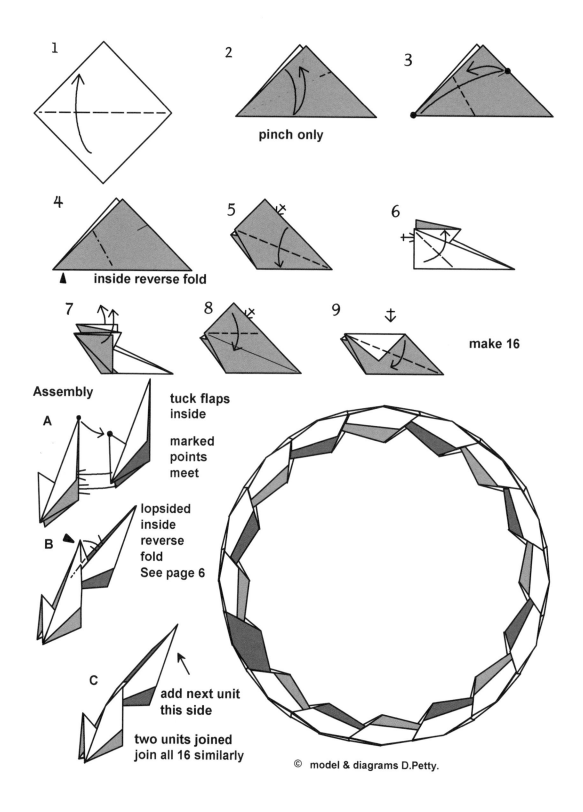

1

2 pinch only

3

4 ▲ inside reverse fold

5

6

7

8

9 ⚓

make 16

Assembly

A tuck flaps inside

marked points meet

B lopsided inside reverse fold See page 6

C add next unit this side

two units joined join all 16 similarly

© model & diagrams D.Petty.

STAR GARLAND 4

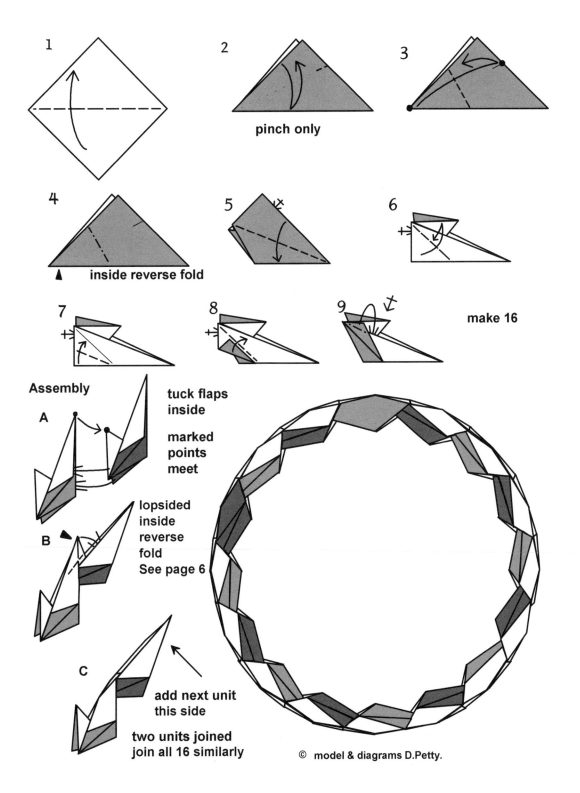

1

2 pinch only

3

4 ▲ inside reverse fold

5

6

7

8

9 make 16

Assembly

A tuck flaps inside

marked points meet

B ▲ lopsided inside reverse fold See page 6

C add next unit this side

two units joined join all 16 similarly

© model & diagrams D.Petty.

STAR GARLAND 5

1

2

pinch only

3

4

inside reverse fold

5

6

7

make 16

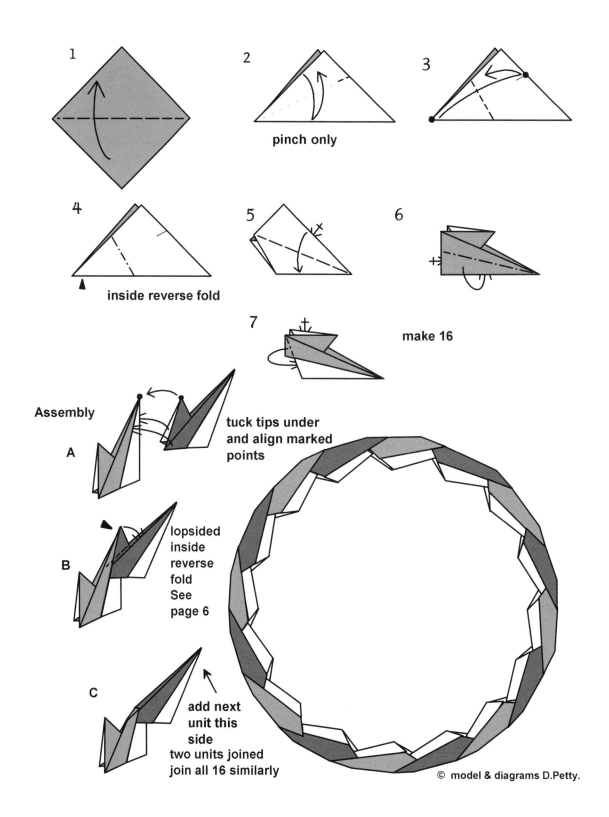

Assembly

A

tuck tips under
and align marked
points

B

lopsided
inside
reverse
fold
See
page 6

C

add next
unit this
side
two units joined
join all 16 similarly

© model & diagrams D.Petty.

STAR GARLAND 6

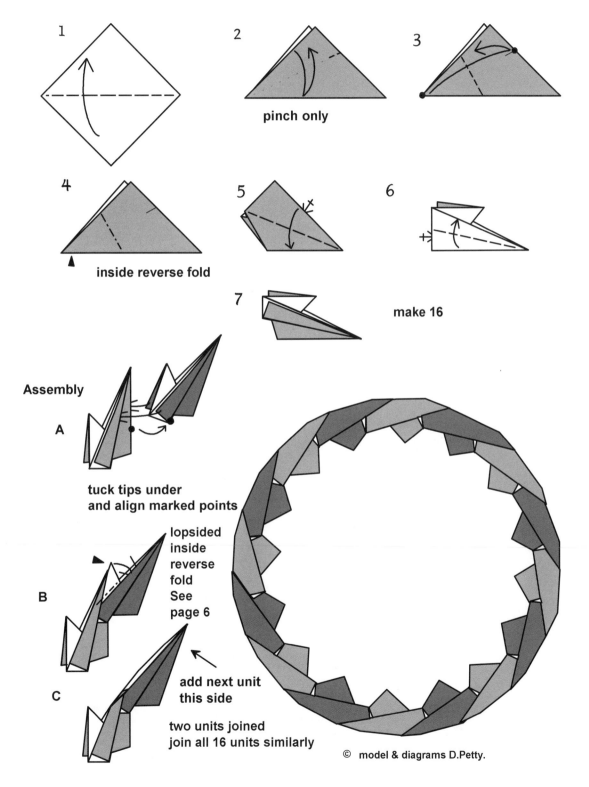

1

2

pinch only

3

4

inside reverse fold

5

6

7

make 16

Assembly

A

tuck tips under
and align marked points

B

lopsided
inside
reverse
fold
See
page 6

C

add next unit
this side

two units joined
join all 16 units similarly

© model & diagrams D.Petty.

FLIGHT OF FANCY

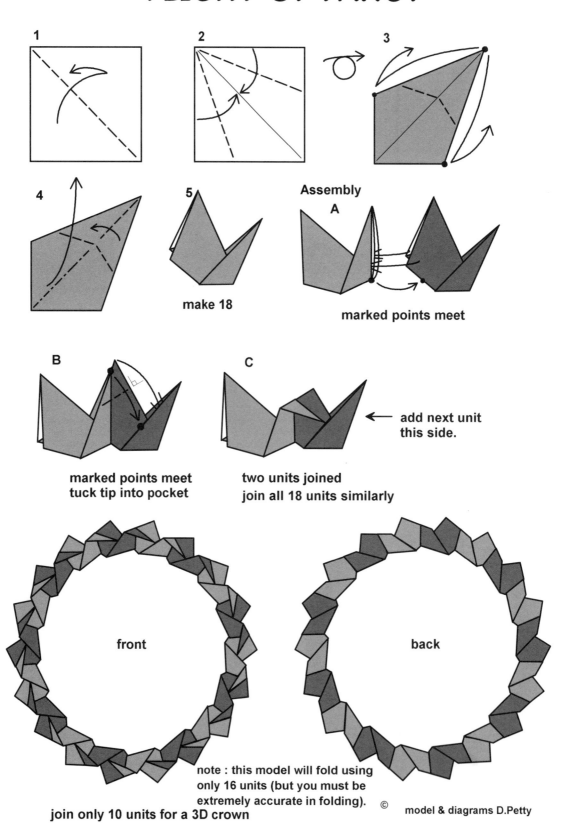

1

2

3

4

5

make 18

Assembly

A

marked points meet

B

marked points meet
tuck tip into pocket

C

two units joined
join all 18 units similarly

← add next unit
this side.

front

back

note : this model will fold using
only 16 units (but you must be
extremely accurate in folding).

join only 10 units for a 3D crown

model & diagrams D.Petty

MARZENE STAR

1

2

3

pinches

4

5

6

Assembly

A

make 8

B

marked points meet

two units joined

join 8, alternating
two contrasting colours

© model & diagrams

D.Petty

Use glue for a robust model

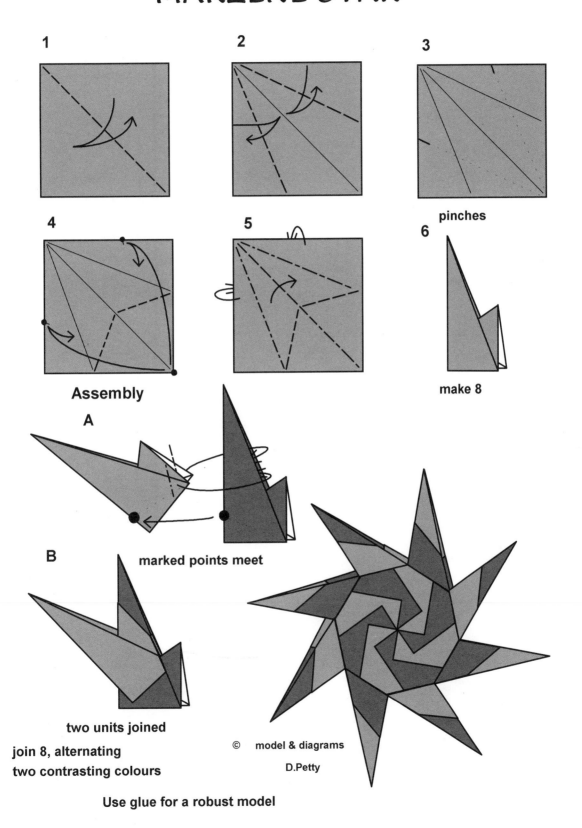

DECADRING

1

fold over 1/3

2

3

4

pull centre flaps

5

fold both together as one
and unfold

make 10
units

Assembly

A

spread apart layers of left unit
to insert right unit

B

both flaps to same side
(X ray view)

Interlock 5 rings to
make Olympic symbol
of red, yellow, blue,
black & green rings.

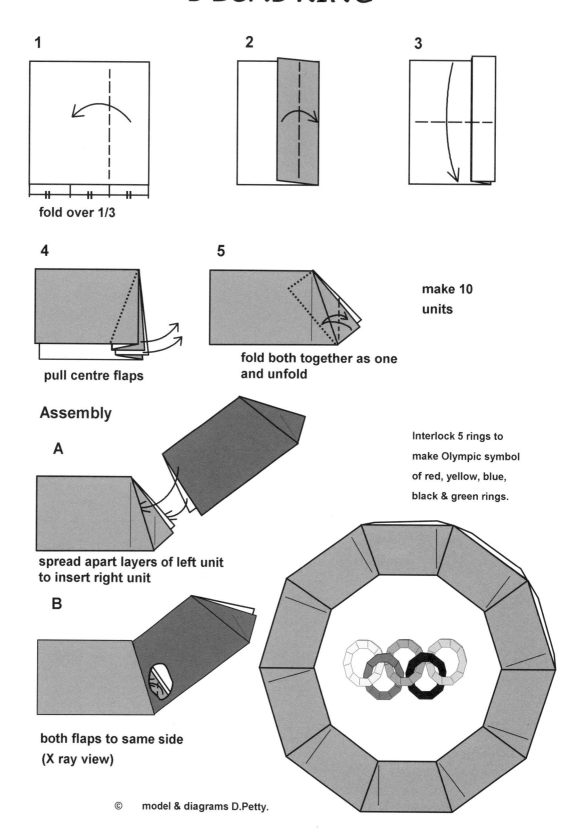

SEPTADRING

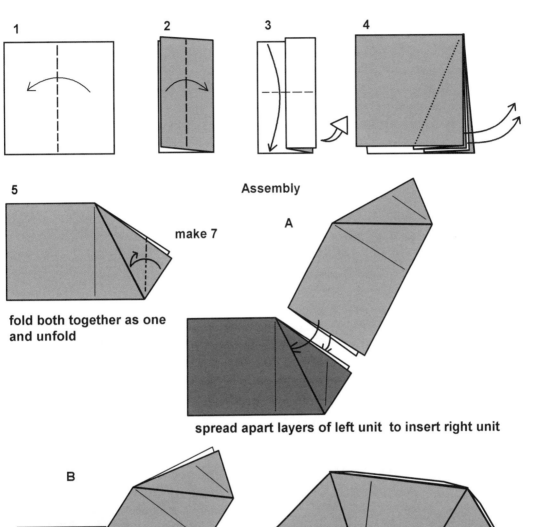

1

2

3

4

5

make 7

**fold both together as one
and unfold**

Assembly

A

spread apart layers of left unit to insert right unit

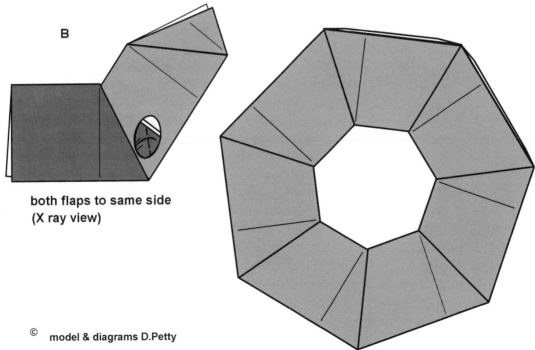

B

**both flaps to same side
(X ray view)**

6: STARS AND WREATHS

MODULAR STAR

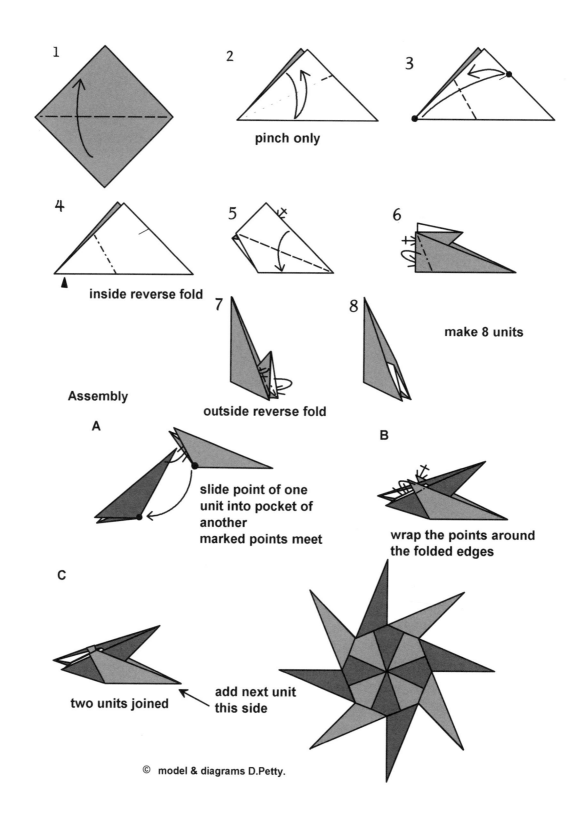

1

2
pinch only

3

4
inside reverse fold

5

6

7
outside reverse fold

8
make 8 units

Assembly

A
slide point of one
unit into pocket of
another
marked points meet

B
wrap the points around
the folded edges

C

two units joined

add next unit
this side

© model & diagrams D.Petty.

MODULAR STAR VARIATIONS

A

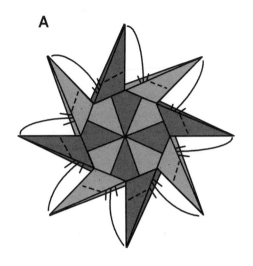

B

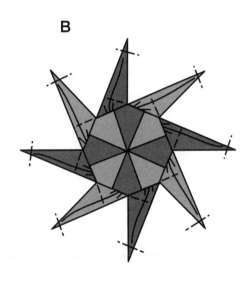

© models & diagrams D.Petty

6: STARS AND WREATHS

*VLIEGENSVLUG UNIT

* (at great speed)

1

2

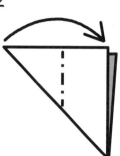

3

**fold oblique
corner, then
unfold steps 2 & 3**

4

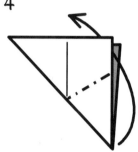

inside reverse

5

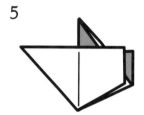

open out

6

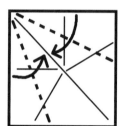

7

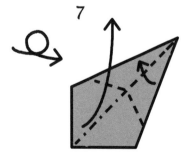

inside reverse

8

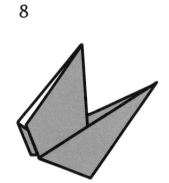

VLIEGENSVLUG 1

Use Vliegensvlug Unit   make 15

Assembly

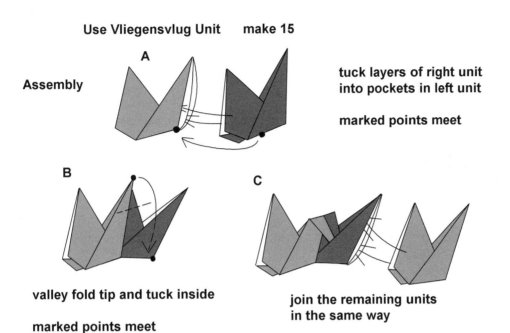

A

tuck layers of right unit
into pockets in left unit

marked points meet

B

valley fold tip and tuck inside

marked points meet

C

join the remaining units
in the same way

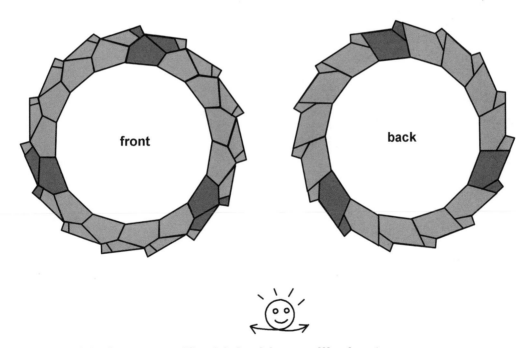

front

back

Decide for yourself which side you like best.

© Model Jose Meeusen

© Diagrams David Petty

WHEEL OF FIRE (VLIEGENSVLUG 2)

Use Vliegensvlug Unit   make 16

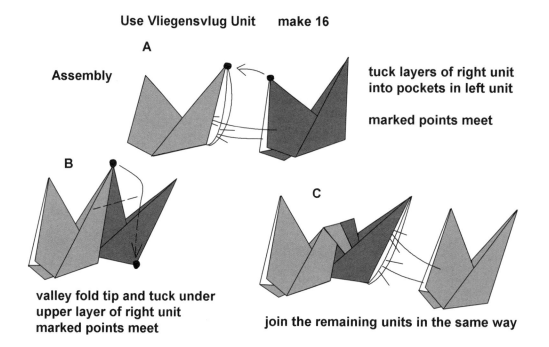

A

Assembly

tuck layers of right unit
into pockets in left unit

marked points meet

B

valley fold tip and tuck under
upper layer of right unit
marked points meet

C

join the remaining units in the same way

Decide for yourself which side you like best.

VLIEGENSVLUG STAR

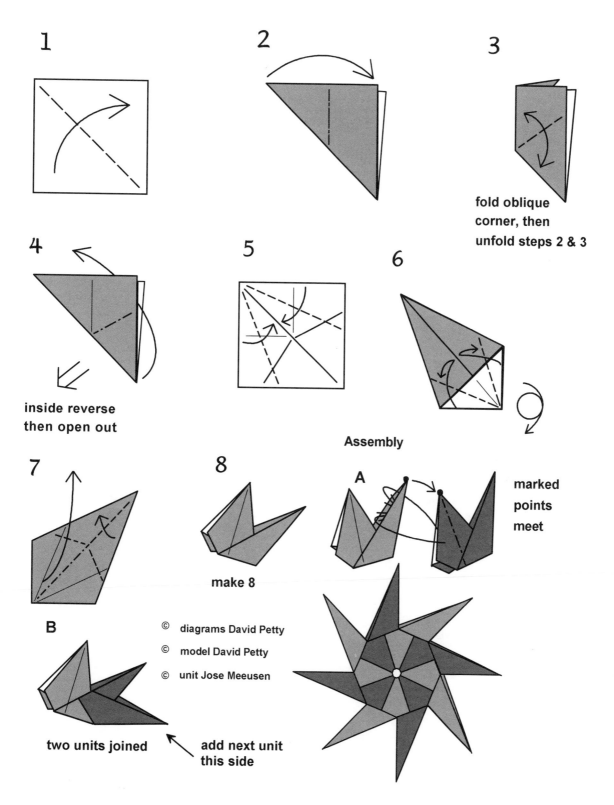

1

2

3

fold oblique
corner, then
unfold steps 2 & 3

4

inside reverse
then open out

5

6

Assembly

7

8

make 8

A

marked
points
meet

B

two units joined

© diagrams David Petty

© model David Petty

© unit Jose Meeusen

add next unit
this side

VLIEGENSVLUG STAR VARIATIONS

A

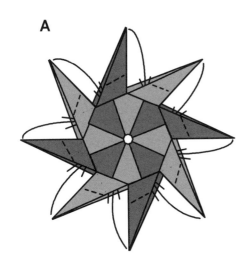

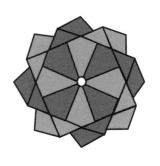

B

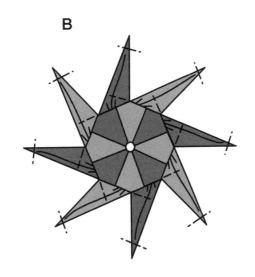

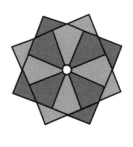

© **models & diagrams D.Petty**

6: STARS AND WREATHS   90

MODULAR CONSTRUCTION

The modular pieces "Ring of Fire" & "Wheel of Fire" can be combined provided they are both folded from the same size paper.

Simply locate "Ring of Fire" inside "Wheel of Fire" as shown in the diagram below. Glue is not required .

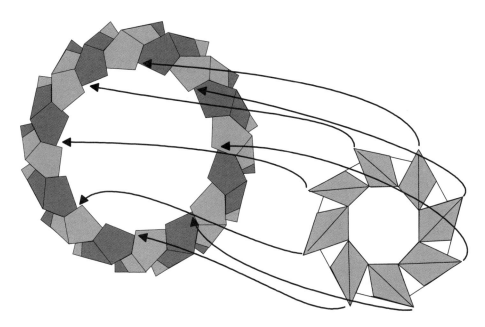

Result.

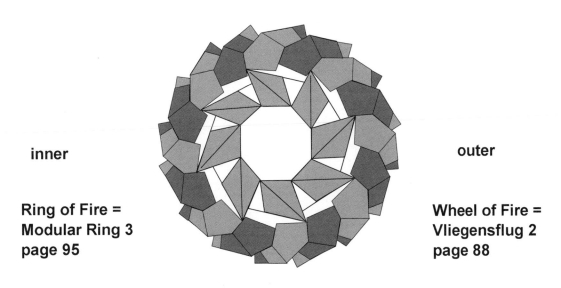

inner

Ring of Fire =
Modular Ring 3
page 95

outer

Wheel of Fire =
Vliegensflug 2
page 88

MODULAR CONSTRUCTIONS

Here are some of the combined modular pieces. Other Modular Rings that can be used in combination with "Wheel of Fire" are: 5, 14, 18, 19, & 21.

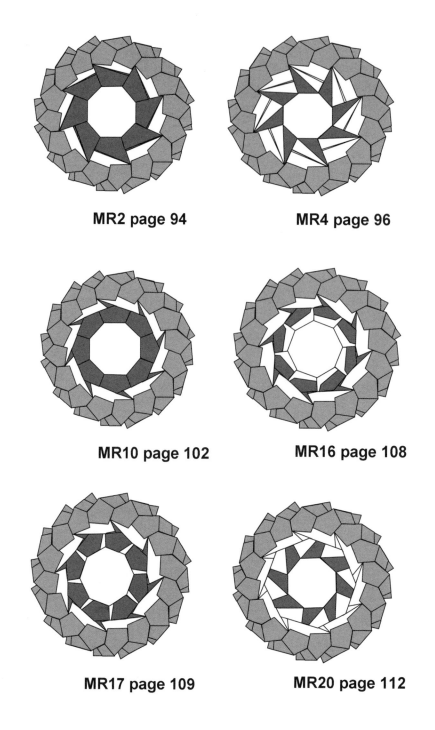

MR2 page 94

MR4 page 96

MR10 page 102

MR16 page 108

MR17 page 109

MR20 page 112

MODULAR RING 1

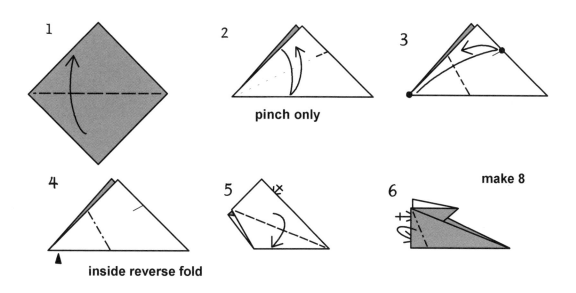

1

2
pinch only

3

4
inside reverse fold

5

6
make 8

Assembly

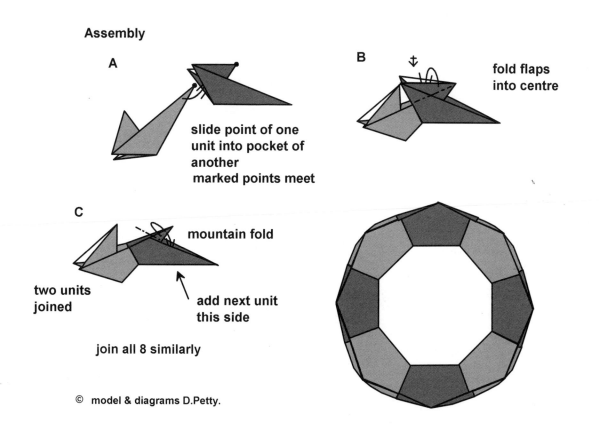

A
slide point of one
unit into pocket of
another
marked points meet

B
**fold flaps
into centre**

C
mountain fold

two units
joined

add next unit
this side

join all 8 similarly

© model & diagrams D.Petty.

MODULAR RING 2

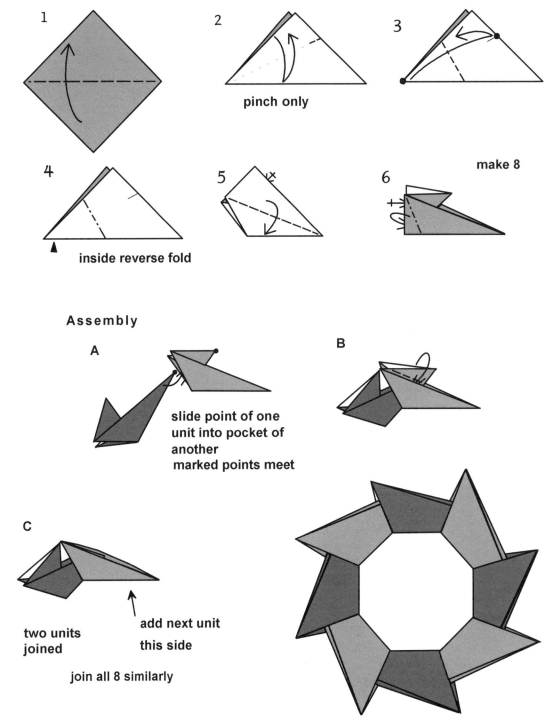

1

2

pinch only

3

4

inside reverse fold

5

6

make 8

Assembly

A

slide point of one
unit into pocket of
another
marked points meet

B

C

two units
joined

add next unit
this side

join all 8 similarly

© model & diagrams D.Petty.

MODULAR RING 3
LAUREL WREATH / RING OF FIRE

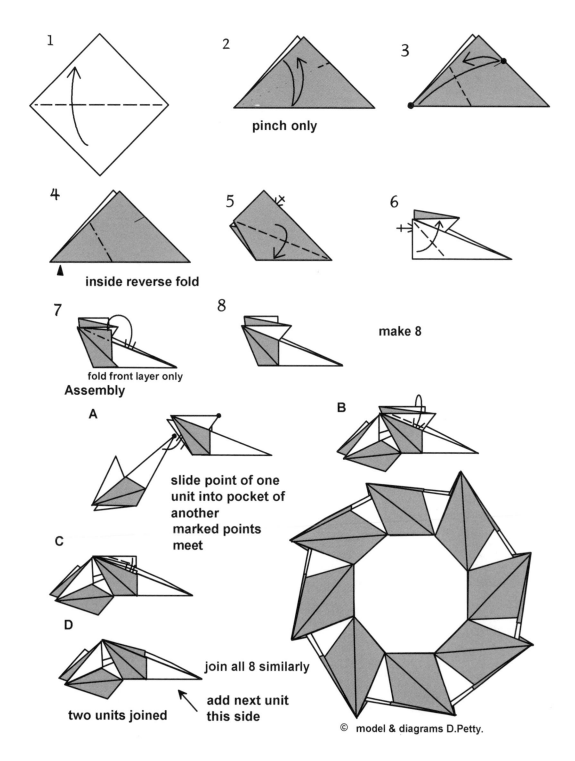

1

2

pinch only

3

4

inside reverse fold

5

6

7

fold front layer only

Assembly

8

make 8

A

slide point of one
unit into pocket of
another
marked points
meet

B

C

D

two units joined

join all 8 similarly

add next unit
this side

© model & diagrams D.Petty.

MODULAR RING 4

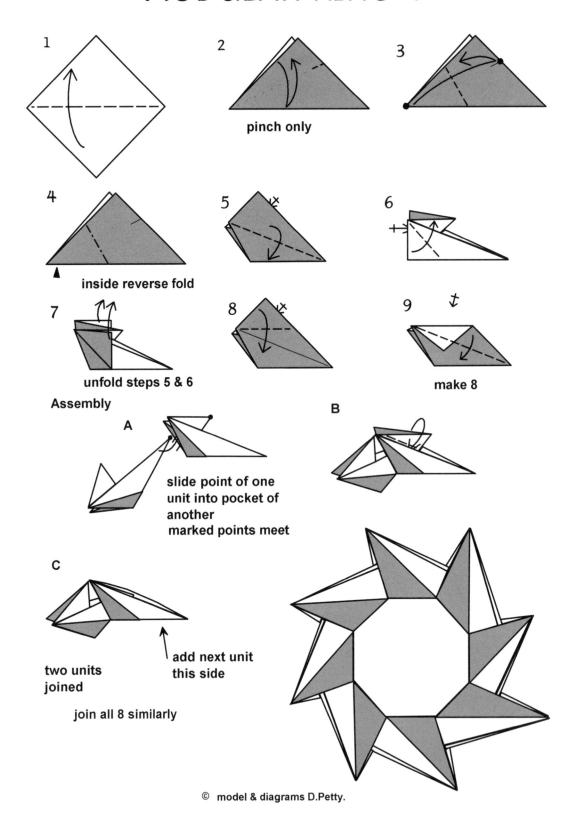

1

2 pinch only

3

4 inside reverse fold

5

6

7 unfold steps 5 & 6

8

9 make 8

Assembly

A

slide point of one
unit into pocket of
another
marked points meet

B

C

two units
joined

add next unit
this side

join all 8 similarly

© model & diagrams D.Petty.

MODULAR RING 5

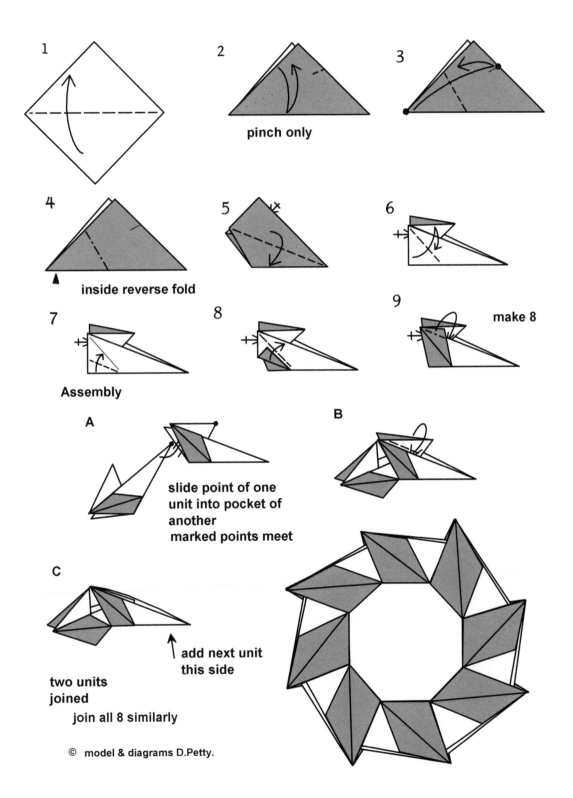

1

2

pinch only

3

4

inside reverse fold

5

6

7

Assembly

8

9

make 8

A

slide point of one
unit into pocket of
another
marked points meet

B

C

two units
joined

add next unit
this side

join all 8 similarly

© model & diagrams D.Petty.

8: MODULAR RINGS

MODULAR RING 6

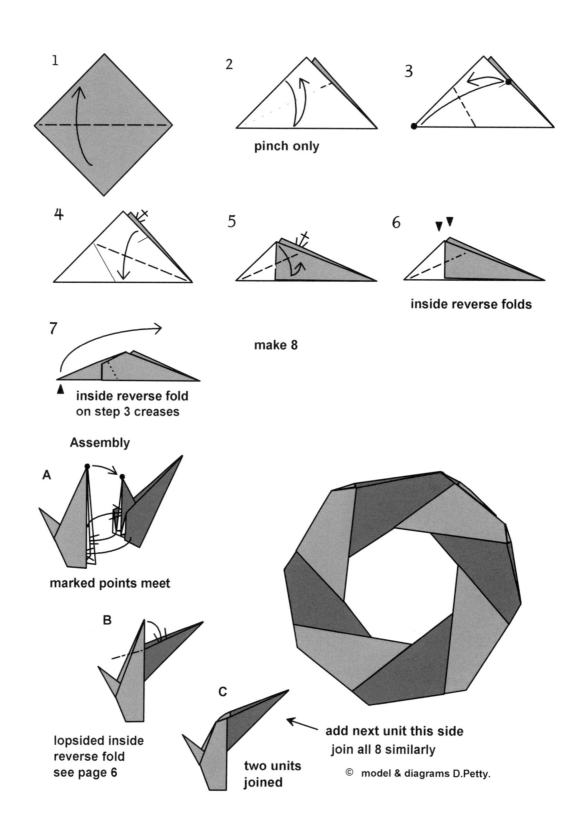

1

2

pinch only

3

4

5

make 8

6

inside reverse folds

7

inside reverse fold
on step 3 creases

Assembly

A

marked points meet

B

lopsided inside
reverse fold
see page 6

C

two units
joined

add next unit this side
join all 8 similarly

© model & diagrams D.Petty.

MODULAR RING 7

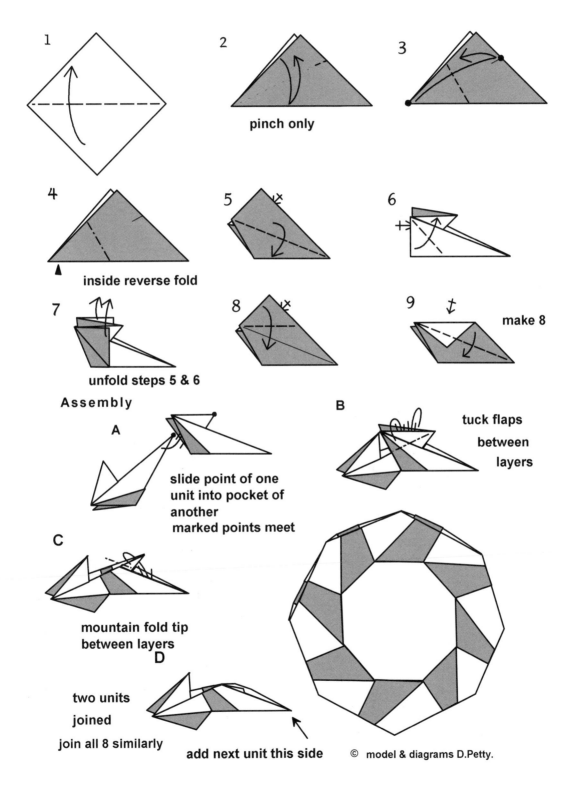

1

2

pinch only

3

4

inside reverse fold

5

6

7

unfold steps 5 & 6

8

9

make 8

Assembly

A

slide point of one
unit into pocket of
another
 marked points meet

B

tuck flaps

between

layers

C

mountain fold tip
between layers
D

two units

joined

join all 8 similarly

add next unit this side

© model & diagrams D.Petty.

8: MODULAR RINGS

MODULAR RING 8

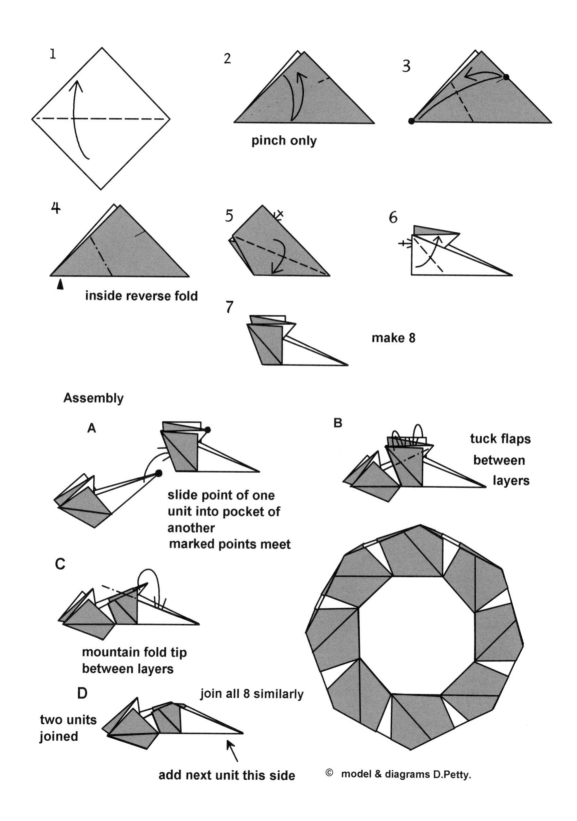

1

2

pinch only

3

4

inside reverse fold

5

6

7

make 8

Assembly

A

slide point of one
unit into pocket of
another
marked points meet

B

tuck flaps
between
layers

C

mountain fold tip
between layers

D

two units
joined

join all 8 similarly

add next unit this side

© model & diagrams D.Petty.

8: MODULAR RINGS

100

MODULAR RING 9

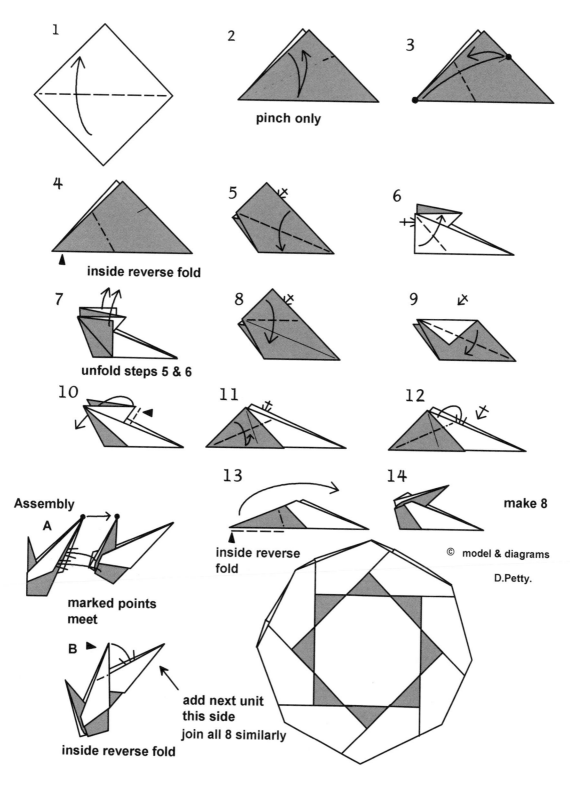

1

2 pinch only

3

4 inside reverse fold

5

6

7 unfold steps 5 & 6

8

9

10

11

12

13 inside reverse fold

14 make 8

© model & diagrams

D.Petty.

Assembly

A marked points meet

B add next unit this side join all 8 similarly

inside reverse fold

8: MODULAR RINGS

MODULAR RING 10

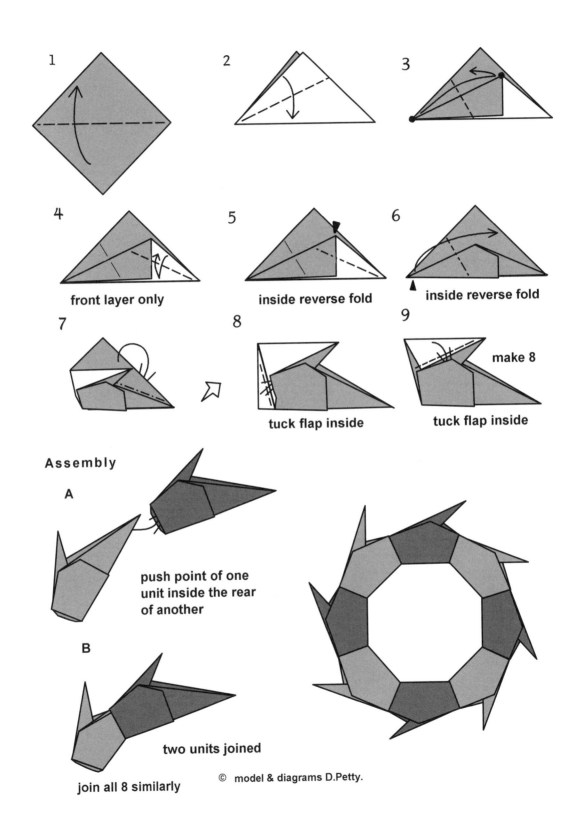

1

2

3

4

front layer only

5

inside reverse fold

6

inside reverse fold

7

8

tuck flap inside

9

make 8

tuck flap inside

Assembly

A

push point of one
unit inside the rear
of another

B

two units joined

join all 8 similarly

© model & diagrams D.Petty.

MODULAR RING 11

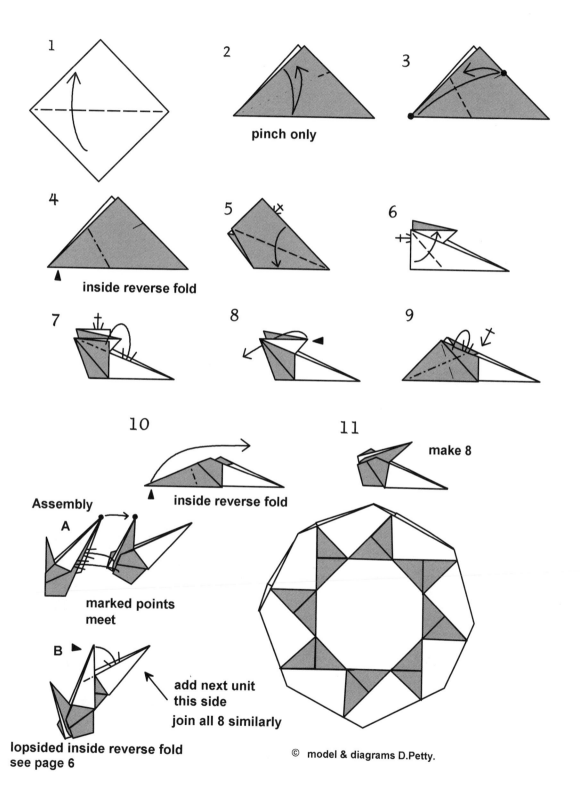

1

2

pinch only

3

4

inside reverse fold

5

6

7

8

9

10

inside reverse fold

11

make 8

Assembly

A

marked points
meet

B

add next unit
this side
join all 8 similarly

lopsided inside reverse fold
see page 6

© model & diagrams D.Petty.

8: MODULAR RINGS

MODULAR RING 12 (flower ring)

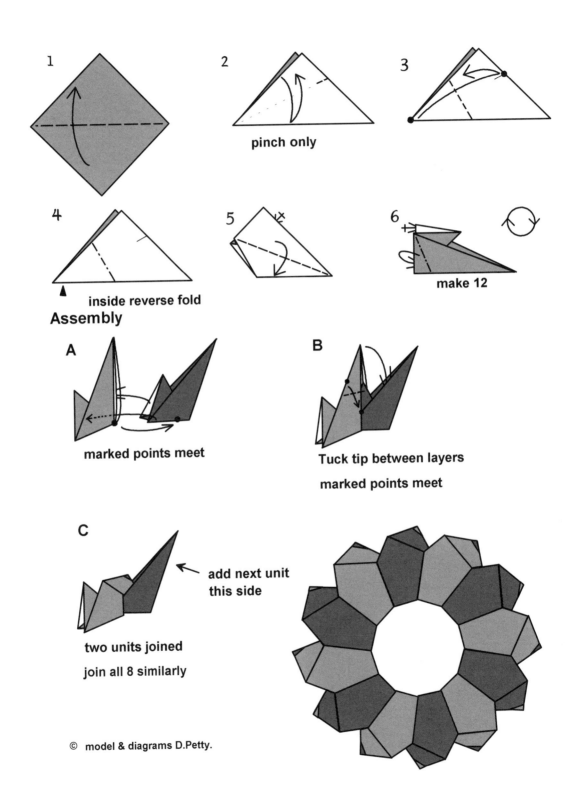

1

2

pinch only

3

4

inside reverse fold

5

6

make 12

Assembly

A

marked points meet

B

Tuck tip between layers

marked points meet

C

two units joined

join all 8 similarly

© model & diagrams D.Petty.

add next unit
this side

MODULAR RING 13

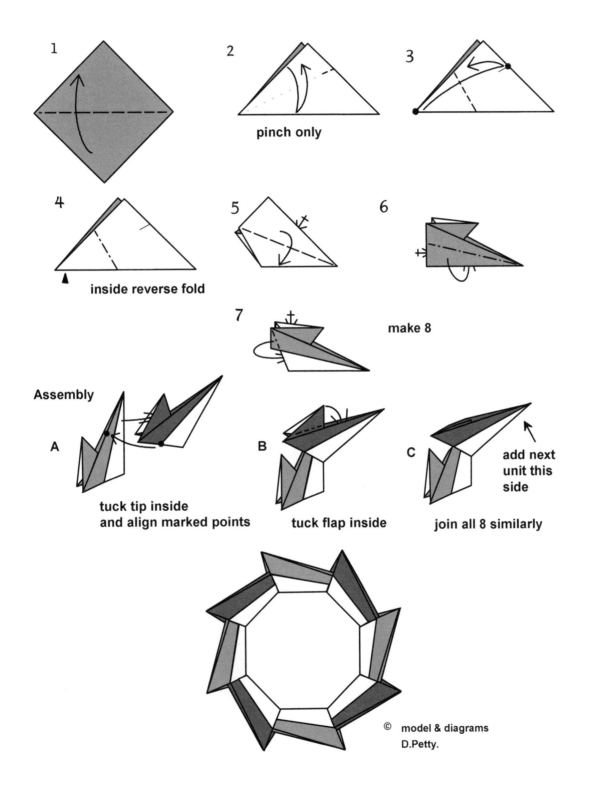

1

2

pinch only

3

4

inside reverse fold

5

6

7

make 8

Assembly

A

tuck tip inside
and align marked points

B

tuck flap inside

C

add next
unit this
side

join all 8 similarly

© model & diagrams
D.Petty.

MODULAR RING 14

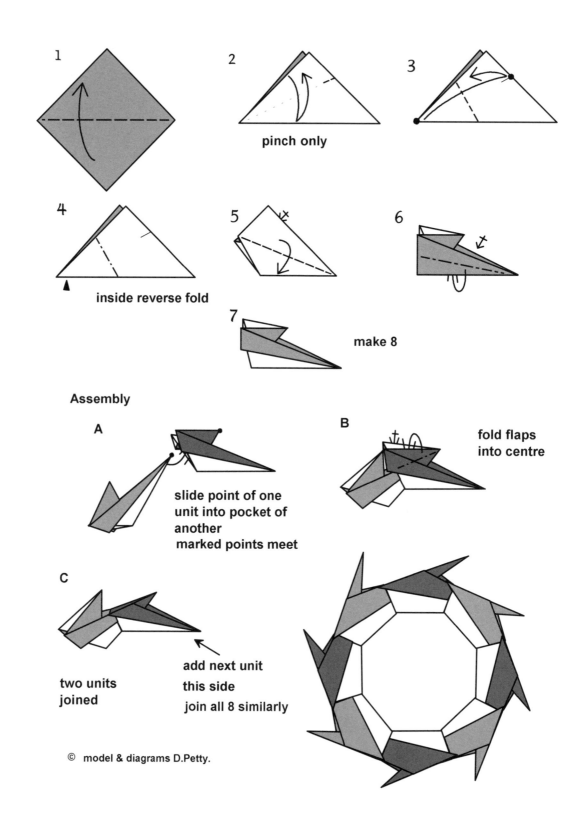

1

2
pinch only

3

4
inside reverse fold

5

6

7
make 8

Assembly

A
slide point of one
unit into pocket of
another
marked points meet

B
fold flaps
into centre

C
two units
joined

add next unit
this side
join all 8 similarly

© model & diagrams D.Petty.

MODULAR RING 15

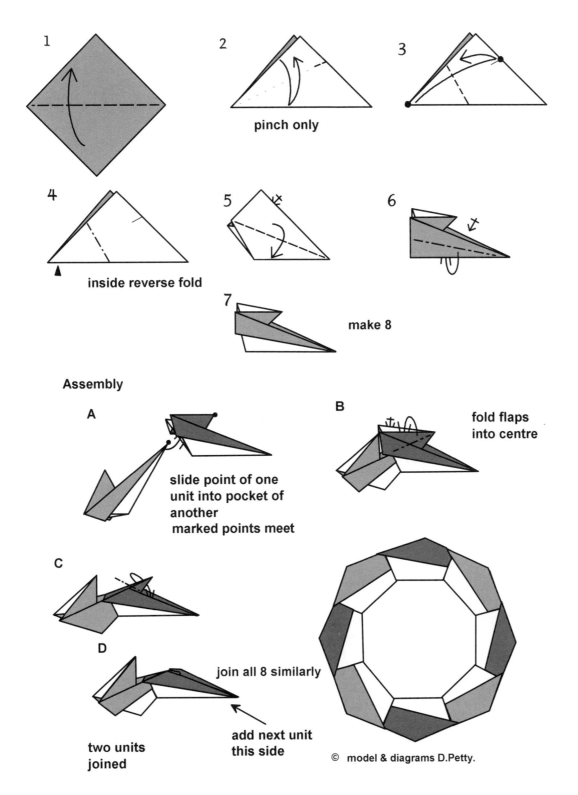

1

2

pinch only

3

4

inside reverse fold

5

6

7

make 8

Assembly

A

slide point of one
unit into pocket of
another
marked points meet

B

fold flaps
into centre

C

D

two units
joined

join all 8 similarly

add next unit
this side

© model & diagrams D.Petty.

MODULAR RING 16

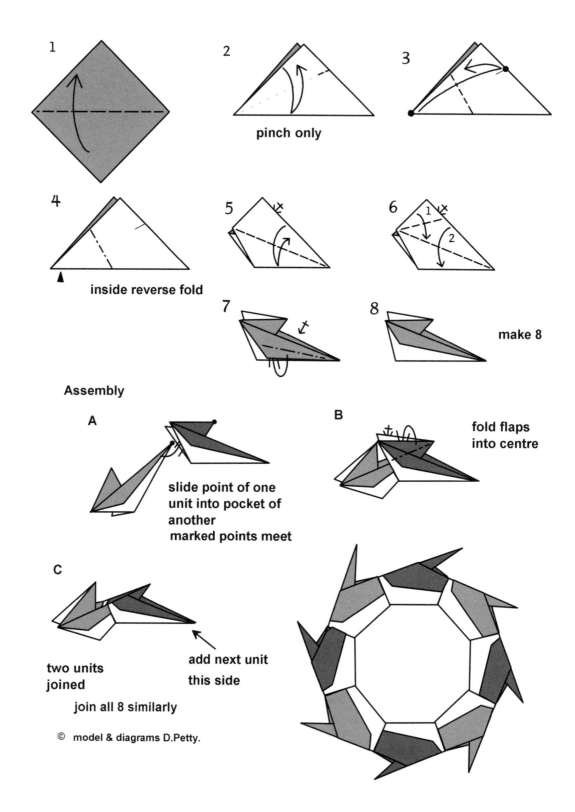

1

2

pinch only

3

4

inside reverse fold

5

6

7

8

make 8

Assembly

A

slide point of one
unit into pocket of
another
marked points meet

B

fold flaps
into centre

C

two units
joined

add next unit
this side

join all 8 similarly

© model & diagrams D.Petty.

MODULAR RING 17

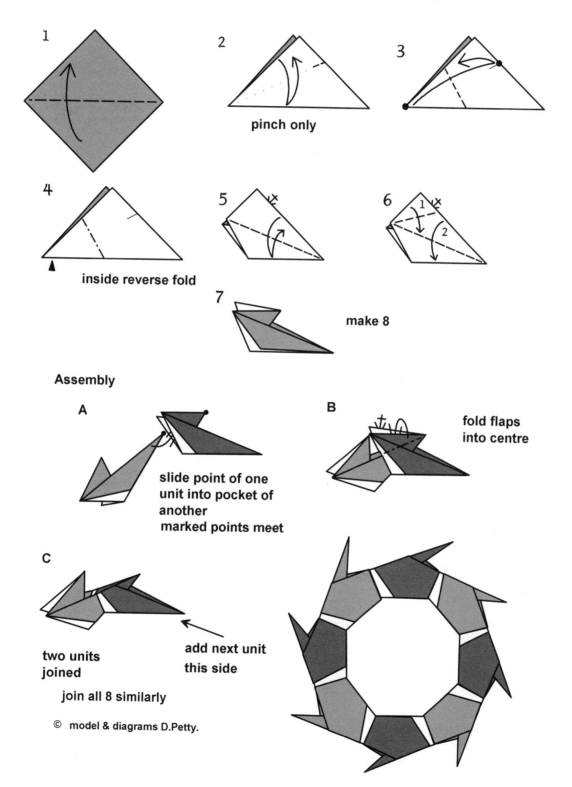

1

2

pinch only

3

4

inside reverse fold

5

6

7

make 8

Assembly

A

slide point of one
unit into pocket of
another
marked points meet

B

fold flaps
into centre

C

two units
joined

add next unit
this side

join all 8 similarly

© model & diagrams D.Petty.

8: MODULAR RINGS

MODULAR RING 18

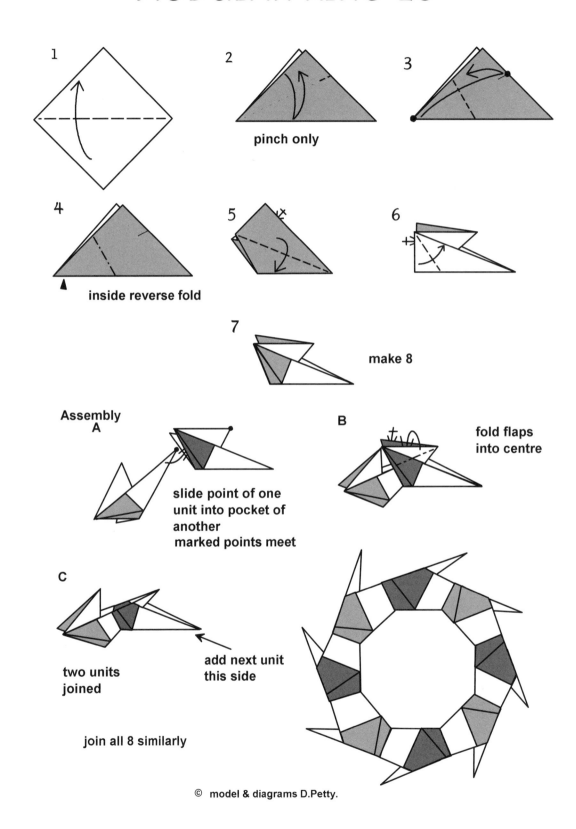

1

2

pinch only

3

4

inside reverse fold

5

6

7

make 8

Assembly
A

slide point of one
unit into pocket of
another
marked points meet

B

fold flaps
into centre

C

two units
joined

add next unit
this side

join all 8 similarly

© model & diagrams D.Petty.

MODULAR RING 19

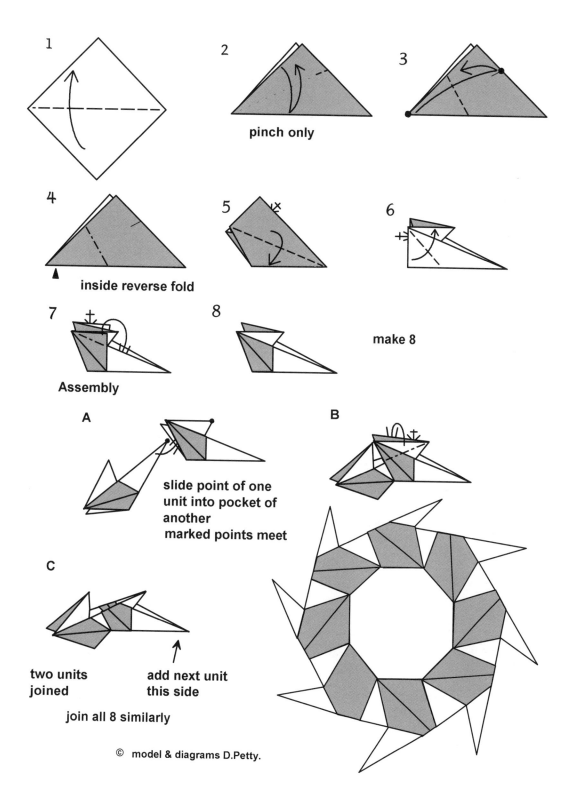

1

2 pinch only

3

4 inside reverse fold

5

6

7 Assembly

8 make 8

A slide point of one
unit into pocket of
another
marked points meet

B

C

two units
joined

add next unit
this side

join all 8 similarly

© model & diagrams D.Petty.

111   8: MODULAR RINGS

MODULAR RING 20

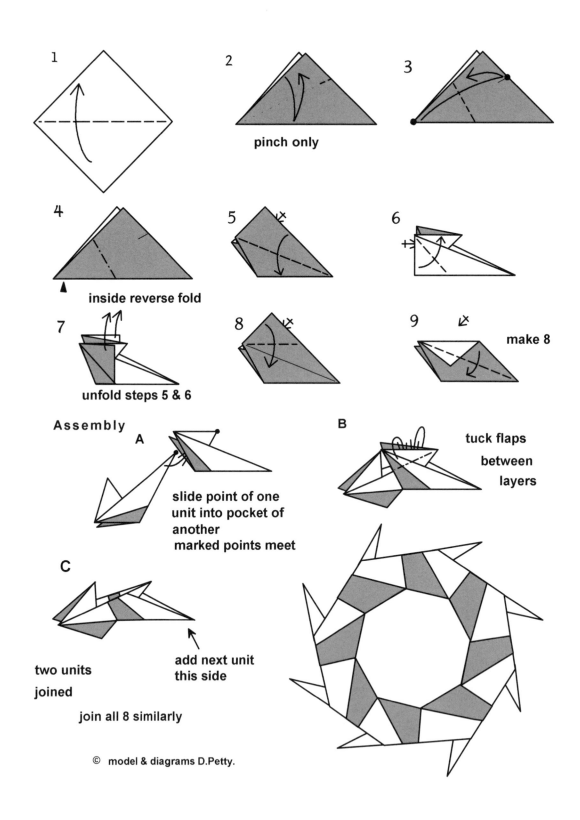

1

2 pinch only

3

4 inside reverse fold

5

6

7 unfold steps 5 & 6

8

9 make 8

Assembly

A slide point of one
unit into pocket of
another
marked points meet

B tuck flaps
between
layers

C
two units
joined

add next unit
this side

join all 8 similarly

© model & diagrams D.Petty.

MODULAR RING 21

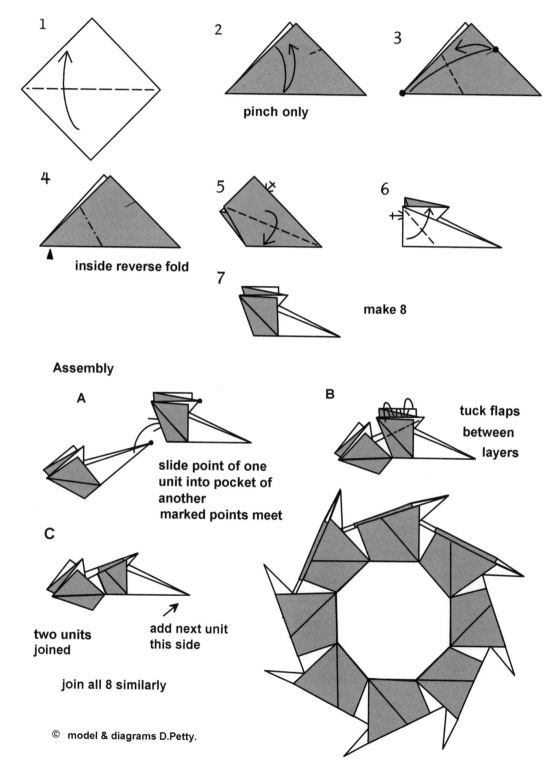

1

2

pinch only

3

4

inside reverse fold

5

6

7

make 8

Assembly

A

slide point of one
unit into pocket of
another
marked points meet

B

tuck flaps
between
layers

C

two units
joined

add next unit
this side

join all 8 similarly

© model & diagrams D.Petty.

8: MODULAR RINGS

MODULAR RING 22

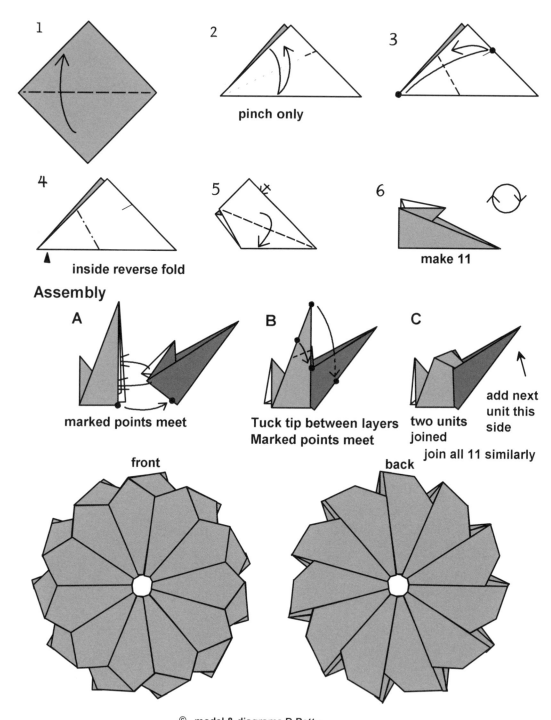

1

2

pinch only

3

4

inside reverse fold

5

6

make 11

Assembly

A

marked points meet

B

Tuck tip between layers
Marked points meet

C

two units
joined

add next
unit this
side

join all 11 similarly

front

back

© model & diagrams D.Petty.

TEACHING MATH LANGUAGE AND CONCEPTS USING ORIGAMI

Origami provides an opportunity for opening up students to the discovery that math is fun, by means of an activity that provides satisfying and tangible results. At the same time it offers practice in carefully following instructions.

Origami is an excellent way to introduce and reinforce math concepts and terms. Paperfolding gives students an immediate hands-on connection to ideas which are new and sometimes difficult to integrate. Finding a line of symmetry or locating a hypotenuse becomes a hunt for landmarks on the treasure map which is a square of paper. The treasure lies in the successful completion of an origami model which may be duplicated and also shared with friends.

Below you will find a sample math lesson to use as a guide in teaching origami to students. This sample lesson is intended as a framework for you to build upon. If material is new to your students you may need to simplify technical terms. More than one class period will be required to complete the model shown in this lesson.

To make sure you understand the folding symbols used in the lesson, begin by turning to the Symbols Section at the front of the book. Before attempting to teach the students, review the section on teaching origami in the Introduction.

SAMPLE MATH LESSON FOLDING VLIEGENSVLUG STAR
by Gay Merrill Gross

Vliegensvlug is a Dutch word meaning at great speed.

Pass out 6 inch origami paper to the students. Hold up a 10 inch square of origami paper and ask the following questions.

• What shape are we starting with? (square, quadrilateral)

• How do we know this is a square? (4 equal sides, 4 equal corners)

• Name the type of corners on the square (right angle corners, 90°) Look for things around the room that have right angles. (windows, doors, blackboard, books, etc.)

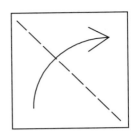

STEP 1: Place paper with white side up on the table and fold one right angle corner to the diametrically opposed (or opposite) right angle corner. Make a fold along the diagonal of the square.

• What is the new shape you see? (triangle)

• What kind of triangle is this? (right angle isosceles triangle)

• Where is the right angle? Where is the hypotenuse?

• Where are the acute angles of the triangle?

• Since we folded two of the right angles of the square in half and these angles were 90°, what is the measurement of the acute angles of the triangle? (45°)

• How does the area of the triangle compare with the area of the original square? (1/2)

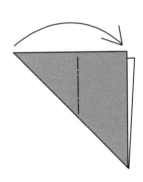

STEP 2: Fold the top acute angle corner backwards to touch the rear of the right angle corner. The crease line formed will be perpendicular to the top edge of the paper.

• What is the length of the top edge now compared to the length of the top edge of the triangle in step 1? (1/2)

• What is the name of the new shape formed? (trapezoid and also quadilateral)

• Can you find the right angle corners? (2 at the top)

• What are the names of the other corners? (obtuse and acute)

STEP 3: Fold the obtuse angle corner in half by folding the lower folded edge to the left folded edge. Crease sharply and unfold. This bisects the obtuse angle. Unfold step 2 and return to a triangle.

• What three shapes are defined by the edges and crease lines on the triangle? (right isosceles triangle, trapezoid, isosceles triangle)

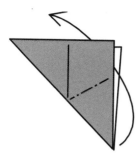

STEP 4: Change the valley crease on the front layer to a mountain fold and inside reverse fold the lower corner in between the front and back layers of the paper.

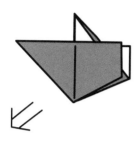

STEP 5: Completely open the paper with white side up.

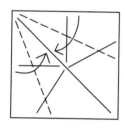

STEP 6: Find the square defined by vertical and horizontal crease lines. Position this inner square so that it appears at the top left of the paper. Fold the left edge and then the top edge of the paper to the diagonal crease line.

• Focus on one of the triangular flaps just formed. What is the name of this triangle? (right angle triangle)

• Where is the hypotenuse? (the side opposite the right angle)

• What is the size of the smaller acute angle ? (22 1/2°)

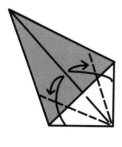

STEP 7: Find the line of symmetry on your paper. Fold each of the white cut edges to the line of symmetry.

• What is the name of the new triangles formed? (scalene)

• What is the name of the overall shape of your paper? (parallelogram) Unfold the triangular flaps just formed and turn your paper over.

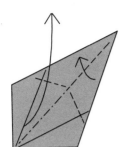

• What is the overall shape of your paper? (quadrilateral)

STEP 8: Find the two crease lines that form two sides of an irregular hexagon on your paper. Refold these two creases as valley folds.

Refold the line of symmetry crease that is within the hexagon as a mountain fold. Refold the line of symmetry crease that is outside the hexagon as a valley fold.

As you fold along these crease lines flattening the paper, you will form an inside reverse fold.

STEP 9: Lay unit flat on table and reinforce all crease lines. Ask each student to fold a total of eight units.

NOTE: a second class period will be required to complete all eight units and the model assembly. Refer to the tips following the lesson for further help in teaching this lesson.

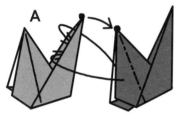

STEP 10: Teach the assembly of the model. Show correct orientation.

Pick up two units and hold them so that the sharp points of each are at the top and on the right. Insert the sharp point of the left unit between the flaps of the right unit. Slide it in as far as it will go, with the two top points touching.

Fold the front flap of the right unit into the pocket of the left unit. Fold the back flap of the right unit into the pocket of the left unit.

Continue to add units. Always add new unit to the right side.

As the eighth unit is added allow it to lay on top of the first unit. After the last unit is attached, insert point of the last unit between the flaps of the first and make the final lock.

TIPS FOR TEACHING THE MATH LESSON MATERIAL
by Laura Lee Hayes

To customize the lesson to elementary grades, you can use alternative ways to describe steps. Simpler words can be substituted in a particular lesson, then built upon in later lessons with other models chosen to introduce more complex terms. You will find that math terms lend themselves to concise and accurate descriptions of each folding step.

To make sure all of your students understand the fundamentals of folding, begin by turning to the Symbols Section and have students practice simple origami moves such as the mountain fold, valley fold, and inside reverse fold.

Any time confusion arises there is an opportunity to back up and describe a second way to see or follow a step, reinforcing the description of shapes with samples drawn on blackboard or cut from paper and displayed as they are discussed. Ask students to look for the shape being discussed on their own paper formed by the fold lines they are creating.

Visual aids are a powerful tool, and you may want to photocopy the model diagram on page 89 onto film for use in an overhead projector. This way the students can follow along with the steps and see the correct results by looking ahead to the next step.

Be prepared to hand out extra origami paper to students who have made a mistake. Mistakes are an integral part of learning. Many new origami models have been invented building upon a mistake. As the paper has value, it is suggested that inviting a student to hang onto the sheet and later play around with it might inspire creativity and encourage recycling.

It is very important to make the initial steps correctly. Discussion of the questions posed in the lesson helps to keep students engaged who have completed a step while others are catching up. As much as possible move only as fast as the slowest student.

Folding the second unit requires a review of the steps for most students. Those students who remember the sequence can help out their classmates and also help you as you work with anyone who is struggling. In helping each other it is very important to ask permission to handle another's paper. Showing them with your own paper is the best way. An adult aid is also very helpful, but be sure the aid understands the material beforehand. Practicing ahead of time makes all the difference in success with teaching origami. Refer to the Introduction in the front of the book .

As it is not possible to complete the model in a single class period, it is a good idea to show only the steps leading up to the completion of the first unit. Once the whole class has completed eight units and is ready to proceed with the assembly of the model, the assembly steps can be shown.

The sample used here has an abundance of mathematical words and shapes to digest. You may tailor a version of this lesson that best suits your students' needs.

ADDED BENEFITS

For middle school students this lesson introduces or reinforces math skills while allowing cross-curriculum activity, practice of hand-eye coordination, and learning to follow directions.

When folding paper, patience is required of both teacher and student as well as careful listening and courtesy. In Japanese culture the importance of respectful behavior is a primary part of life, which carries over into the ancient art of origami.

There are other opportunities to discuss the international scope of origami, the chance to communicate beyond spoken language. The model has a Dutch name because the creator of the unit is from Holland, while the author of the book and creator of the model is an Englishman. The story of how these two people came together is in the Biographies Section on the next page.

STUDENTS WITH SPECIAL NEEDS

Students often make a smooth, more relaxed integration and application of math concepts from interaction with a hands-on approach. This is especially true of dyslexic students or those with various learning impairments, due either to emotional or physiological handicap.

Physically handicapped students are able to handle simple folds, when given the extra time and positive support required. This gives the satisfaction of having successfully completed a task they have done themselves, thus building confidence and perseverance.

For blind students, careful use of language, repeating each step and one-to-one assistance will allow them to explore origami from their own perspective. To help students struggling to "see" a step, encourage them to put their hands on yours and experience the process. Let them also feel the result on the paper. Wherever possible reorganize the folding sequence so you are folding to an edge of the paper. This is an easier landmark to find and to fold to than a crease in the paper.

BIOGRAPHIES

David Petty

I work as a semiconductor process engineer, and have a degree in mathematics and physics. I first came across origami in 1981. My wife, Lilian, bought an origami book, "Origami 1 - the Art of Paperfolding" by Robert Harbin, to teach at a local youth club. After folding all the models in the book I wrote to the address (in the city of Birmingham, 50 miles away) given in the book. A reply came from the village next to our home town of Hazel Grove. Soon after I met the writer and former secretary of the British Origami Society (Dave Brill) and joined the Society.

I have creations in several areas, but my main ones are pleated models, heart models and modular or unit models. I've diagrammed other folders' work as well as my own. The BOS booklets "The Genius of Jan Willem Dirksen", "Paper People and Other Pointers", "Modular Construction and Twists", "Index of (BOS) Convention Models" & "Making Faces" are to my name. The Dutch Origami Society (OSN) has also published a collection of modular pieces "Unit Origami". I've also produced a book of heart models titled "Hearts 3D". I have had models exhibited and published in most countries. I am the current secretary of the British Origami Society.

I first met José Meeusen, a Dutch lady, when working on a project in Holland. A small group of Dutch folders used to meet once a month. The leading light was Marc Overmars who at that time was producing a periodical called "The Origami Collection". A large part of the models printed in the collection were taken from those meetings.

José was producing original models at that time. The acquaintance has lasted, mainly because of similar folding interests and shared origami friends. José has had work exhibited and published in most countries. She has several books, all origami related, published in Holland, with subjects ranging from greetings cards to doll clothes. She has contributed several booklets for the OSN (the Dutch Origami Society).

One of the main chapters in this book "Celtic Brooches" was initiated by the receipt of her original model "Vliegensvlug". My badly observed drawing, sent in response to the original, turned out to be a new model "Vliegensvlug 2" and this eventually led to the creation of the rest of the family. I give my heartfelt thanks that José gave her permission to publish her models in this book, the inclusion of which has made the content richer by far.

My first acquaintance with Gay Merrill Gross was made when she came to London to the 25th anniversary of the British Origami Society. She is the author of several origami books published in the U.S. Gay teaches origami and mathematics in the New York city area. She is part author of an origami and mathematics book "Step-by-step Projects that Teach across the Curriculum". She readily volunteered to contribute an example math lesson, for which I am very grateful.

David Petty

José Meeusen

I am José Meeusen (also known as José Krooshoop). I was born in The Netherlands in 1948. As I child I was always busy reading, cutting, folding. After finishing secondary school I wanted to become a kindergarten teacher. During those studies I learned about the education and folding methods of Friedrich Fröbel.

In the early eighties I found a picturebook about a simple piece of paper that turned into an elegant swan through paperfolding. The diagrams of that beautiful model were included, so I tried to fold it. I was immediately fascinated by the wonderful art of origami.

I became a member of the Dutch Origami Society, which gave me the opportunity to obtain books and paper. I folded as many of the models as possible, the more complicated the better. Soon I started to teach origami at the school where I worked. I was asked to give courses to adults, elderly people and children. My youngest student ever was only 3 years old and the oldest 78 years old. The most important thing of my teaching was to let the students experience the pleasure of folding.

In 1990 I was asked to make my first origami book. So far I have made 6 books. In the meantime I also began designing geometric models.

In 1991 Origami Deutschland organized their annual *Origami-Ttreffen* in the Fröbel museum in Germany. This meeting opened a whole new world for me as a teacher and as a folder. I met designers from other countries and I learned about new origami opinions and theories. I made lots of new friends and it was the beginning of a considerable correspondence with folders all over the world. This gave me the opportunity to broadcast my models. Their enthusiasm was - and still is - very encouraging to me. My models have now been published in many countries like Great Britain, France, Germany, Japan, Hungary, Spain, Israel, U.S.A. and of course The Netherlands.

I have great respect for the paper and the possibilities it provides. After designing a lot of simple models, following the usual scenic (step by step) routes, I found that there must be far more ways to create a nice model. I started to investigate new moves, utilizing folding techniques and the quality of the paper. I began designing abstract, geometric models.

When I am designing I do not know beforehand what I am about to make. I just start making some creases and I will see what I can do with it. I always try to find new, interesting and surprising moves. When I have finished a first rough copy I unfold it and try to find out which creases are really necessary. I prefer neat models that do not have a lot of unnecessary creases at the surface. It is also important to make use of all the paper. I do not like hiding flaps that are "left over".

For me origami is more than just a craft or skill. I can express myself in designing models. Origami can also be therapeutic. I find folding and designing models relaxing.

José Meeusen

RESOURCES

SUPPLIERS: If you have difficulty obtaining paper locally, then mail order supplies can be obtained from:

FASCINATING FOLDS
P.O. Box 10070
Glendale, AZ 85318
 USA

http://www.fascinating-folds.com
tel: 800/968-2418

ORGANIZATIONS: If you enjoyed this book and want to know more about paperfolding then try writing to the addresses below:

ORIGAMI USA
15 West 77th Street
New York, NY 10024-5192
USA

BRITISH ORIGAMI SOCIETY
Membership Secretary
2a The Chestnuts
Countesthorpe
Leicester
UK

ORIGAMI SOCIETEIT NEDERLANDS
Mossinkserf 33
7451 XD
Holten
Holland

If you are curious to learn more about David Petty's work, go to his website at

http://members.aol.com/ukpetd